YOUNG'UNS

Other books by Celestine Sibley

CHILDREN, MY CHILDREN

JINCEY

SMALL BLESSINGS

DAY BY DAY WITH CELESTINE SIBLEY

SWEET APPLE GARDENING BOOK

MOTHERS ARE ALWAYS SPECIAL

ESPECIALLY AT CHRISTMAS

A PLACE CALLED SWEET APPLE

DEAR STORE

CHRISTMAS IN GEORGIA

PEACHTREE STREET, U.S.A.

THE MALIGNANT HEART

CELESTINE SIBLEY
YOUNG'UNS

A CELEBRATION

1817

HARPER & ROW, PUBLISHERS, New York

Cambridge, Philadelphia, San Francisco, London
Mexico City, São Paulo, Sydney

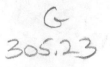

FIRST EDITION

Library of Congress Cataloging in Publication Data

Sibley, Celestine.
   Young'uns: a celebration

   1. Children—Georgia. 2. Parent and child—Georgia.
I. Title.
HQ792.U5S54   1982   305.2'3'09758   81-47676
ISBN 0-06-014953-1   AACR2

82 83 84 85 86 10 9 8 7 6 5 4 3 2 1

For
Jimmy, Susan, Mary, John, Charles,
Sibley, Ted, Susy, David,
John Steven
and also Edward and Ron

YOUNG'UNS

A few years ago there lived in the north Georgia mountains a man I sometimes think of when the subject is children. Our friend Herbert Tabor told us of this gentleman, and, looking back, I wonder if it was mere coincidence that he usually thought of the story when he would see my children and their friends swarming over his strawberry patch like a plague of locusts or with their feet under the table in his kitchen wolfing down hot rolls and Mrs. Tabor's homemade preserves.

According to the story, Mr. Tabor's father, judge of the Court of Ordinary of Gilmer County, walked home from the courthouse to lunch every day and often got in a little work in his garden before he returned to his office. He was hoeing his beans one day when a countryman from up in the hills walked up, dragging in his wake a string of dirty, runny-nosed little children.

"Jedge, I want to talk to you," the visitor said.

"Well, make haste," said the judge. "I got to finish this row of beans and get back to the courthouse."

"What I want to ask you, Jedge," said the man, "is, Do you want some of these young'uns?"

"No, much obliged," replied the judge, continuing his hoeing. "I got about all the children I can clothe and feed and send to school."

"I figgered you'd say that!" the man shouted, triumphant in his disgust. "I been to the mill and the mine and the lumberyard, and there ain't a soul that wants any of my young'uns. All I got to say"—he raised his voice and shook his fist furiously—"all I got to say is it's a damned sorry place where you can't give away a young'un!"

The desire to give away a young'un may have struck me from time to time, but only fleetingly. My three and their nine, counting two little ones who died, have been . . . well, I'll tell you: While I was in the hospital recovering from the birth of my third child, my employer, the late famed *Atlanta Constitution* editor Ralph McGill, sent me a lovely little cache of cologne and dusting powder, not for the baby but for myself. With the gift came a note inquiring, "Haven't you found out what's *causing* 'em yet?"

"Causing what?" I asked the friend who delivered gift and note. I was genuinely puzzled.

"Babies, dummy," she said, laughing.

I was weak and tired from baby-having and may be excused the hours I wasted brooding over Mr. McGill's cheerful inquiry and nurturing hurt feelings. Surely he knew that having a baby was a magical, wonderful thing, not something to be brushed off like a case of hives? Surely he knew that to give birth was a woman's highest calling?

When I got my strength up enough to walk into his office I put those questions to him. He was surprised that his little joke had fallen with such a thud. And apologetic. Indeed he did value babies. Indeed he did think birth a miracle and motherhood the greatest blessing. To salve my wounded feelings he took me to lunch and then, realizing belatedly that a new mother wants not a gift for herself but something for her baby, he stopped at a bookstore and bought my little daughter her first book of poetry.

Later I was to see that the great editor understood fully about the joy and pain of children. His wife, Mary Elizabeth, who had been denied babies by a series of physical maladies and lost an adopted daughter to leukemia, finally conceived. McGill was on a trip around the world for the American Society of Newspaper Editors when his son was born. He was returning and had got as far as Hickam Field in Honolulu when Frank Wells, then a young naval officer, now a veteran reporter for the *Constitution*, handed him a message sent by his waggish associate Jack Tarver.

The message read: BABY BOY, WEIGHT SIX POUNDS SEVEN OUNCES, BORN CESARIAN, 8:24 A.M. WEDNESDAY, APRIL 25. LOOKS LIKE YOU BUT IS HEALTHY.

As Harold Martin wrote in his affectionate biography, *Ralph McGill: Reporter,* the editor's life "thereafter was unashamedly to revolve" around his son.

For a considerable chunk of their lives, most parents find themselves in the same boat, all their efforts bent to provide for and care for their children, all their hopes and fears and love and worry focused on what a renowned Georgia Supreme Court justice called "children, the seed corn of the future." With Bacon, most of us can say, "Children sweeten labours but they make misfortunes more bitter."

What do we get in return?

A few years ago, impelled to write a column for Mother's Day, I expressed the wistful wish that the beribboned packages which most of us would get could contain our most wanted and needed gifts.

Patience, I decided, may be the greatest package life can hand a mother—patience and humility and a listening heart. So many of the years that you are a mother you spend talking when you should be listening, you spend railing out when you should be quiet, you spend advancing your ideas when you might be examining theirs. If some Mother's Day when your children are very small, I mused, you could open a little ribbon-tied package that contained patience . . . ah, what a gift that would be!

At the same time I contemplated the gift that most children give you willy-nilly: stretch.

Once I interviewed an engineer who specialized in bridge building. He had in his spare time invented a "stay-up-top" girdle which was enormously successful. The idea of an engineer designing a girdle amused me, but he was very casual about it.

"Why not?" he asked. "It's just another matter of stress and strain."

Knowing girdles perhaps more intimately than he did, I thought there is also the problem of stretch. Stress, strain, and stretch. Girdles and children.

When the word "latex" hit the language, everything in the world seemed to have "stretch" built into it. But there's nothing that guarantees stretch in the human heart and mind. Some of us lose our rudimentary flexibility as the years pass, becoming victims of rigidity of ideas and attitudes. But children help, they do help.

I think I began to be aware of that when my firstborn was a month old and I took him for his initial visit to the pediatrician. In those days people dressed up to go to a doctor's office. I dressed up the baby, not myself. Just as if he were not going to be stripped and examined in nothing but his own rosy hide, I stuffed his little body into the most thoroughly tucked, embroidered, lace-edged, beribboned things his new layette had to offer. He was bathed and powdered within an inch of his life and finally enveloped in a gossamer-soft handmade fringed carriage robe. I didn't realize until hours later that I had forgotten to comb my hair, had lost my lipstick, and left home without a coat, although it was a particularly chilly January day.

Six years later when that baby was a first-grader and had spent his first summer in day camp, I was reminded afresh of the surprising roles into which children cast us. At the camp closing exercises Neal Baxter, the director, said genially, "Will the mothers of the Black Panthers please stand?"

Black Panthers had not gained the notoriety then that would subsequently be theirs, but still . . . I hadn't known I was the mother of any kind of panther! I looked across the room at my skinny redheaded little boy and I choked—with amusement and amazement. Could he be a Black Panther and I the mother of a Black Panther?

It was one more tip-off to a lifetime of surprises—of stretch, if you will.

It was inconceivable to me when Elvis Presley was starting out that any full-grown woman with walking-around sense would go forth in the broad open daylight and sit in the front row of a theater to watch his, to me, obscene gyrations and to listen to him bawl out songs about blue suede shoes and hound dogs. I went.

My daughter Mary and her best friend, Mary Em, had

saved their spending money to buy tickets. When I couldn't dissuade them I wouldn't allow them to go by themselves. Afterwards I even went backstage like any fool fan to speak to the young man with the greasy duck-tail haircut and let the little girls shake his sweaty hand.

Stretch? To the point of snapping! But it was good for me. I knew what people were talking about years later when the singer died and a large portion of the populace went crazy with grief. I was also prepared for the Beatles when they came along.

A life-sized cardboard effigy of Eddie Fisher inhabited the downstairs closet of my house for a time, startling our cleaning woman out of her wits and causing her to put on her hat and shake the dust of our house off her feet—at least, temporarily.

When his owner, my middle child, Susan, finally relin-quished Eddie, taking him out and setting him on the gar-bage can for pickup and ultimate ignominious disposal by the city, we recognized it as a milestone in her life. As her younger sister said, she was no longer in love with card-board Eddie. She had found a real live love.

Naturally I saw circuses I would have missed, if it had been up to me, spent hours on the sidelines bobbing my head encouragingly at swimming classes, piano and trom-bone lessons, dance recital rehearsals. I, who had never learned to dance properly, found myself buying tutus and ballet slippers, a rapt spectator at the *Nutcracker* and *Swan Lake.* I, who had no knowledge of and only the meagerest appreciation of music, found myself bringing home from the library records and librettos so my music-loving children would know what it was all about when we went to the Metropolitan Opera. Elaine May and Mike Nichols were spoofing when they mentioned Andre Kostelanetz as the peer of classical music, but I didn't laugh. I thought he was—until my son introduced me to Bach fugues.

Reared in the country, I believed dogs and cats properly belonged out of doors. My children persuaded me otherwise. My life sometimes seemed centered in the housebreaking of a series of animals. They not only occupied my house but often my bed.

My daughter committed me to drive her and a group of her fellow Girl Scouts to a Saturday outing at Camp Timber Ridge. I went willingly, taking a book to read and an apple to eat in case I had a long wait.

"Oh, you're not supposed to *wait!*" one of the little Scouts admonished me. "You're supposed to take us on a nature walk and *show us things!*"

My impulse was to take off through the tall timber, leaving the little girls to see "things" for themselves or to call on some expert. My daughter's eyes on me held me in check. I didn't know much about what the nature walk had to offer, but I found I knew more than I thought I did. And that afternoon's outing opened up to me a field that has been a lifelong delight. I now take nature walks because I want to. I even read books—on my own time—about bugs and rocks, trees and wildflowers.

Friends are often unwittingly "stretched" by one's children. A bachelor friend of mine who took me to a cocktail party at Atlanta's fashionable Piedmont Driving Club was horrified later to remember that he had—at the starry-eyed urging of one of my daughters—walked up to the guest of honor, sequin-suited pianist Liberace, and asked for his autograph!

For years, when reminded of it, my urbane friend would either deny it or insist that his sensibilities had been dulled by the consumption of several double martinis. Then he married and became the father of many children, and what he had considered as unthinkable and outrageous shifted into perspective. He has done many more improbable things under the pressures of parenthood, I am sure.

You read books you didn't know you were interested in, including the imperishable adventures of Dick and Jane and their dog, Spot. You make things you had no idea of ever needing, clown suits and Billy Goat Gruff suits and the inevitable Christmas wise man's robe and turban out of old curtains. I, who considered the Civil War over and done with when the last Confederate veteran died, have visited every battlefield between Atlanta and Gettysburg, following along in the wake of my son, who still calls it "The War for Southern Independence" and decorates his room with pictures of General Robert E. Lee.

Educational? Sure. I remember saying, "Jimmy, I thought *we* won the battle of Gettysburg," and his somber reply summed up that and all wars: "Mama, nobody won."

You may be a recluse by nature, loving time to yourself, savoring aloneness, but when you have children you meet the neighbors, you go out to see people, you *socialize*—oh, nasty word. You meet the neighbors because your children have already met them. My daughter Mary, at the age of one year, found her way to a neighbor's apartment and was in the kitchen raiding the refrigerator when our search party caught up with her.

Our city neighborhood, where we lived the seventeen years the children were growing up, ran mostly to older people who had moved there when it was opened up before World War I. Some of the elderly couples appeared so reserved and unreceptive to newcomers that I didn't dream of becoming obligated to them for more than a passing greeting. How was I to know that they would rescue my children from passing trucks, buy their weight in Girl Scout cookies and school carnival tickets, ransack their attics for costumes and props for plays, show up to ply me with coffee and reassurance when my youngest was missing for five hours? (That was the year of the widely publicized death of a little girl named Kathy Fiscus in an abandoned well, and naturally I figured Mary, with her talent for catastrophe, had found an old well to fall into in downtown Atlanta.)

Obligated? I owed neighbors not merely boundless gratitude but carfare and lunch money they supplied in emergencies.

Drunks and jailbirds and picturesque street vendors were not unknown to me, a newspaper reporter, but I was not prepared for teenagers I would meet, feed, welcome to our bed and board. There were boys called Swine and Wild Man, Fingers and Brother James and Brother William, who worked on greasy automobiles in my driveway and argued over the relative merits of trumpet players Harry James and Bunny Berigan in the kitchen, all the while consuming quantities of whatever food the pantry offered.

There were little girls who brought sick hamsters to

visit, practiced the violin, toppled vases and ashtrays with their baton twirling, and writhed and stomped and yelled in preparation for cheerleading tryouts.

Oh, I met people, I sure did, including teachers I went forth in fear and trembling to see, and an assortment of other parents who, like me, toiled out in bathrobes and housecoats at 4 A.M. on Sunday to deliver the newspaper which on that day was too big to fit in the bicycle baskets of our carrier sons.

I met entire theatrical troupes and occasionally turned over my bed to an old actress or a young dancer who happened to be "between engagements." My daughters were stagestruck, of course, serving as faithful little back-stage props and scenery acolytes to whatever summer theater production would have them. I had always enjoyed live theater, but I doubt if I would ever have sat through weeks of rehearsal and six nights of performance of *The King and I,* if I hadn't been a mother. Anna Mary Dickey was great as Anna, it happened, but I was there because my daughter Mary, her hair dyed the most sinister black with shoe polish, had snagged a role as one of the king's children.

I grew accustomed to seeing what little furniture we had go out the door and show up later on the stage in *Tobacco Road* or *The Potting Shed* or *A Hatful of Rain,* whatever play had sets so shabby our stuff was usable. An early-to-bedder by nature, I found myself staying up late to wait out scene shifting and to join cast and crew in after-the-play postmortems. One summer a downtown motel offered its pool to the company, and since I couldn't very well enforce a curfew on my daughters at such a time, I went swimming with them. Even then, floating on my back and contemplating the city's night sky, I marveled to find myself in such a place at such a time. A motel swimming pool at 2 A.M.? It seemed a very odd place for me to be until a veteran actress named Georgia Simmons, then in her eighties, went splashing by wearing my very best bathing suit, which my daughters had graciously lent her.

Georgia was the most flexible person of any age I had ever encountered. Her curiosity, her openness to new experiences, new people, were a marvel to me. Once when she was close to ninety years old she was on her way by Greyhound bus from Hollywood, where she had played the old grandmother in *Face in the Crowd*, to New York, where she lived, and she met a girl who was going to Las Vegas. Georgia changed her ticket and went with her. She had always heard of "Vegas," she said, and it was a priceless opportunity to take a look at it. Our friendship with her, which began the summer she played Ada in *Tobacco Road*, was to continue for many years, the direct result of my children's venturing into the world of the theater.

Pushing a stalled car anywhere never has been a novelty to me, but pushing a car down Peachtree Street with jazz pianist Marian McPartland was certainly unexpected. I might have gone out to interview Miss McPartland, who was in town to give a concert, but I wouldn't have asked her and her hostess, the late Lila Kennedy, home with me if Jimmy hadn't been her worshipful fan and bedazzled at the idea of meeting her.

Wouldn't you know the car would conk out in traffic and the star, who is delightfully flexible herself, would climb out and help me push while Lila steered? Jimmy's pleasure at meeting and hearing one of his all-time jazz idols was matched by my pleasure in learning of one of her personal, purely private projects. Wherever she goes Miss McPartland quietly, with no fanfare, no publicity, arranges to give a concert for retarded children. Little ones who are locked into silence, and are unable to communicate with the world in general, respond remarkably to music, especially music as played by Marian McPartland. I slipped in through the back door to one of these musical mornings, and when I saw the faces of the children and watched their clumsy efforts to pat their feet and clap their hands in time with the piano I realized that my jazz fan at home had an instinct about quality people which certainly surpassed my own.

The civil rights storm broke over the country in the 1950s, and although I was alternately interested and shocked, sympathetic and frightened, it was from the position of a spectator. I took no part in it. My fourteen-year-old daughter did.

She had joined forces with a group of older teenagers who were meeting on campuses, picketing lunchrooms, marching down the streets of Atlanta carrying placards, boldly confronting the Ku Klux Klan which, placarded and berobed, came out to meet them. Proud of her idealism and her bravery, I was also terrified. Later, when she ran away from summer school, where she was making up a history course she had flunked, I was wild with apprehension and anxiety.

She had gone, I learned from her friends, to join Dr. Martin Luther King, Jr., in Montgomery—headed as surely for Mississippi's Parchman Prison as if she were an old and hardened criminal, I thought.

Years later, when she was grown and married and had two children, I was to recall that time with pain and a sharp sense of poignancy.

My five-year-old grandson John and I were driving across Alabama and Mississippi to Shreveport, Louisiana, to make an Easter visit with her, his aunt, and his cousins. It was a dark rainy night, and after a hamburger stop in Montgomery, John went to sleep on the back seat. We had reached Mississippi, and the rain was beating against the windshield and the lightning was flashing wildly across the sky. Static had made me turn off the radio, but it was lonesome in the black rainswept night, so I fiddled with the dial, hoping for news. I got a fragment or two about a shooting somewhere, before the crack of lightning and the roar of the wind and rain let the whole story through.

Dr. Martin Luther King, Jr., had been shot in Memphis!

The lights of a truck stop were just ahead, and I pulled off and sat there. The impulse of all newspaper reporters is to call the office when news of great moment happens, to ask, "Do you need me? Shall I come in?" But I was more than three hundred miles away with a sleeping child on the back seat and other children ahead waiting for me. The need for any services of mine would be over by the time I could get back, so I sat there by the Mississippi truck stop, watching the rain make mud of the parking lot, watching the big trucks pull in to wait out the rain and thinking about Dr. King, that kind man, that eloquent man. Gone.

My personal acquaintance with him was slight. He had done me a favor once. That day Mary had left school and caught a bus for Montgomery, I had called Dr. King.

I was frightened, I was frantic. With his own people being beaten and killed, my concern for my little white child might well have amused him. It didn't.

"She's got to *learn* history before she can *make* it!" I wailed. He agreed. He said he would find her and talk to her, and within a few hours one of his aides took her to the Montgomery airport, boarded a plane with her, and brought her home.

Sitting there by the truck stop, I wished that I had been as eager to do something to help his cause as my child had been. I wasn't even sure I had said thank you to him.

Many people who are reared in the church depart it when they grow up and get married and move away from home. I did. But if you were reared in church and value it, the time will come, usually when you have children, when you think about returning. I began to think of finding what the ministers call "a church home" when my children were babies. I had been reared between the Presbyterian church in Mobile and what was handiest, the Methodist Sunday school and once-a-month sermons of a circuit-riding Methodist minister in the country. My husband's family were divided between Southern Baptist and Episcopal. Many of my girlhood friends were Roman Catholic, and the Jesuits' fine school, Spring Hill College, was the only one close enough for me to attend by a five-cent streetcar ride during the Depression. So I also had Catholic leanings. I decided to shop around.

Oddly enough, no church we visited seemed to be "it." Many were beautiful and welcoming. I made good friends in several denominations. But none latched on to my heart and seemed to minister unto my needs.

My son was attending North Avenue Presbyterian Church's day camp with a friend, and one day he said, "Mama, if we're going to church, let's go to that one."

The very next Sunday we went, and it became one of the most comforting, sustaining associations of my life. The psalms and the old hymns, the first poetry in the lives of many of us, delighted me. The Sunday morning sermons, unlike some I had been hearing, seemed addressed to my needs, my failings, my aspirations. I never listened to them without feeling determined to try harder, to do better, to aim a bit higher. Entering that quiet and reverent place on Sunday morning with the light streaming through the stained-glass windows and the organ playing softly, with my children rustling ahead or behind me in their churchgoing best, I usually felt an easing of the week's accumulation of tension, a calming of anger and frustration, the beginning of serenity. My children loved the church and the friends they made there when they were little, and then they reached adulthood and, like me at that time of life, wandered away, to return later, I hope.

Not long ago my younger daughter mentioned one of the happy times of her childhood as the hour before bedtime when I read to them, shared cocoa and cookies, and ended with family prayer. I remembered it happily too, and I didn't think to remind her that it was her idea in the first place. She came home from visiting a Sunday-school friend and asked, "Why don't we family-pray?"

I honestly hadn't thought of it. I knew it was a custom in many homes, but it had never been in ours. We had gone to bed carrying with us the tiredness and the bickering and disappointments of the day. I was often in violation of the old admonition, "Let not the sun set on your wrath." We would, I promised, give it a try.

It wasn't always easy. Finding time for it was sometimes difficult. Often when it came their turn to say a prayer, the children would air their grievances in what a minister friend of mine called "horizontal praying."

"God, please make Mary leave my best underpants alone!" Susan would pray.

And Mary's supplication would come hard on: "For Jesus' sake make Susan stop being so hateful."

But mostly it was a little time of quiet when we were together and mindful of the blessings we shared. Maybe the airing of the complaints—prayerfully, as it were—was beneficial too.

Of course it's nothing to have a baby. Millions of people . . . well, okay, what is more wonderful? Absolutely nothing can touch the suspense, the excitement, the wonder of birth. I don't care what I say from time to time.

Getting ready for a baby is part of it. My mother picked up in the country the expression "raking straw." A woman approaching childbirth was compared to an animal moving serenely about pushing hay or straw into place for the accouchement. The way most of us rake straw is to paint furniture or wash slipcovers or climb up on stepladders and scrub woodwork, all things we are told by our doctors and older women in the family not to do, all things we can't seem to help doing.

Before my first baby was born my mother arrived to spend a month, bringing her trunk with her (one of the last trips that old trunk was to take before it was retired). She had it packed with dozens of handmade dresses, gowns, robes, and receiving blankets and bolts of bird's-eye converted to hand-hemmed diapers. She had embroidered and tucked and whipped on miles and miles of lace. Neither of us found out until later that babies do very well with just undershirts and diapers, and hardly anybody strains their eyes with shell-stitch edging any more. You learn that with second babies, not the first.

Muv walked miles with me every day to strengthen my muscles for the delivery room, and she alternately frightened and enthralled me with country lore about baby-having. If you "carried the baby high," it was a boy. Or maybe a girl, I forget which. If you looked on ugly or frightening things, you "marked" the baby. There's always a tale about a woman who saw a frog or an alligator and gave birth to a child which either resembled a frog or alligator or had the likeness of one in a birthmark somewhere on its body. Mothers-to-be were admonished not to "work over your head," the danger being that the umbilical cord would stretch and choke the baby. (After the first baby, even believers paid no attention to that. There were too many diapers to hang on the clothesline.) The part I liked was, of course, the happy signs and influences. If you remained calm and tranquil you'd have a good-tempered baby. (I did.) If you thought beautiful thoughts, looked on lovely things, listened to music, and read poetry, your child would have a sunny disposition, an innate love of beauty. (Mine did.) You were indulged in your "cravings," maybe for the only time in your life. I developed a yearning for hot apple pie at midnight, and fortunately my husband knew a bakery which pulled diminutive two-person pies out of the oven at precisely the hour he finished the night shift at the newspaper. Also fortunately, it was not good form in those days to tell a pregnant lady to watch her weight.

Anyhow, just before Christmas—and a Christmas baby is a very special baby, of course—Jimmy was born. The maid of my best friend and next-door neighbor heard the news, asked the baby's sex, and cried out in delight, "Oh, I am so glad! I know she is proud, for that was her desire!"

I was proud. That *was* my desire. My mother thought producing that baby boy was the handsomest performance of my life. She stayed long enough to ruin the pediatrician's schedule, which in those days was rigid. You didn't just pick up a baby any old time and hold it. There were "hours" for cuddling.

"What does *he* know about babies?" Muv demanded. "I bet he doesn't even have one!"

And she picked up Jimmy when he cried and petted and rocked him when he or she felt like it. By the time our second baby was born, the cycle of baby-having wisdom had turned, there was a new term, TLC, tender loving care, and rocking and cuddling at all hours were "in." I came to be glad that Muv's wisdom was not cyclical but steady and unchanging, and before our family was well into babies I found myself accepting what early on had been taboo—thumb-sucking and walking the colic, among other things.

After Jimmy came the girls, Susan and Mary, and everybody in the family agreed that was a gracious plenty. We had enough children, all we could manage—more than we could manage, sometimes.

When Georgia's U.S. Senator Richard B. Russell was being talked up as a candidate for president back in the 1950s, I did a series of stories on his childhood and growing-up years. I spent a lot of time in the wide-verandahed old white frame house in Winder where his mother still lived.

She was a bright and interesting lady, then in her eighties, and I wondered how she had survived with such grace and good humor the rearing of nine children.

"Didn't they bicker and fight and get into things and drive you crazy?" I asked one day.

She shook her head.

"Mine do," I said.

"How many children do you have?" she asked.

I told her three, and she smiled broadly.

"My dear, you have six too few," she said.

What I lacked in numbers could only grieve me a little while. In almost no time at all my children were having children. We were starting all over. There were seven grandchildren in all and then a gap and two more. The surprising thing to me was how ever-new the experience was. We never seemed ready or calm about any birth. The sense of urgency, the fear, the expectancy were as sharp and fresh with the last as they had been with the first.

There were times when I thought the suspense of the second-to-last grandbaby would kill me. Mary had quit her job and gone home to get everything in readiness. She and her husband, Ron, had bought a dilapidated, falling-down house in an old section of town with the idea of shoring it up and restoring it. The baby-to-be's room was dark and cheerless, and for a time my other daughter, Susan, Mary, and I were happily engrossed with paint and new white linoleum for the splintery floor, with organdy curtains and ruffled pink gingham cushions and comforts for the hand-me-down crib. Mary packed her suitcase, and she and Ron attended classes to get him, at least, ready for the big event. (It was his first baby.) Beside her suitcase there was a little tote bag which was to hold a sandwich, a candy bar, and perhaps a beer for him if the delivery, in which he was to participate, dragged on and he had time for a break.

Everything was set, except that the baby would not come. I called night and morning and swung by on the way to work. I took daily looks at the little room and then inspected my daughter searchingly. Was she being purposely slow? Maybe she wasn't well. That bloom . . . was it health, or could it be she was feverish? I urged brisk walks and then got scared and urged her to stay by the telephone.

One morning I hurried by Mary's house to see what I might see. What I saw was Ted, whose birth had been an event fifteen years before, sitting in front of his aunt's television set.

"What are you doing here?" I asked. "Where's Aunt Mary?"

"Cars," said Ted. "My dad's car wouldn't start and my mom's heater isn't working and she had Susy's car pool and they were going by Mrs. Singleton's to swap cars with her. . . ."

He was off on one of those interminable logistics discussions that we know well in this family: who has what car where and who is going to pick it up. There was something about Aunt Mary going with his mama to pick up a car somewhere.

Finally, I'd had enough.

"Why aren't you in school, and is the baby coming?" I demanded.

"Well, I've been sick but I can't miss any more days," he said, snuffling his nose dramatically. "So I was going, but my mom's car—"

"Never mind about the cars!" I cried. "What about the baby?"

"What baby?" said Ted. "Susy has gone with Mom and Aunt Mary. It was her car pool."

"Not Susy!" I yelped. "The new baby, the *new* baby!"

"Oh, yeah, that's right," said Ted. He looked longingly at the television set. "Maybe that's where they are now. They've been gone an hour. Could you have a baby in an hour?"

"A baby in an hour?" I shouted. "Oh, Ted!"

I called the hospital, but they had never heard of our baby so I went on to work. Five days later, Ron called me. The baby had decided to arrive.

Naturally, I felt that I was needed at the hospital, and naturally I was not. After a while Ron came out of the delivery room with the word that things were slow and I was to go on to the office. At my desk I didn't seem to focus my attention on anything. When the phone rang I hurried the caller off the line, saying, "I can't talk now. I'm having a grandchild."

When people dropped in I said distractedly, "I've got

to hurry now. I'm having . . . my daughter's having . . . *the baby is coming!*"

To do them credit, nobody said, "What baby?" They acted as if there were only one, a unique and important baby, and they tactfully acknowledged my responsibility to get there. So I went back to the hospital.

The service I performed was perhaps not spectacular. I sat in what is called the Father's Waiting Room, only fathers seldom wait there as they did in former times. They don gown and mask and scrub up and stand by in the delivery room. I grabbed anybody passing by and asked, "Our baby . . . is it here yet?"

What kept happening was that they thought I was talking about *their* baby, and they would give me a report complete with dimensions as if they were talking about Miss America. When I caught on that they were talking about the wrong baby, I decided to help by calling up people. I called Alexandria, Virginia, to tell the baby's other grandmother that I was there on the job and that the best information I could get from the delivery room was that "things are coming along nicely."

Before she thought, Jean, my Virginia counterpart, said, "I've got to hang up now. I'm expecting—" Then she laughed and said, "I've been doing that all day. What is the word?"

You'd have to be a genius to make the only word I had, "Things are coming along nicely," endlessly interesting. And endless was the time Mary had been in the delivery room.

Seven hours, eight hours, nine hours.

Susan came bringing paper cups of coffee and date cookies. She was cheerful and optimistic. For an hour or two. Then she began to pace the corridor and rummage for dimes to call up people.

She was of a mind to go into the delivery room and tell her sister to hurry up in the peremptory way she used to yell, "We gon' be late for school! Don't you dare take my sweater!"

Then the doctor and the baby's father came through the swinging doors looking in their aqua gowns and caps as if they were on the way to a costume party.

"A boy," they said.

We jumped around and hugged one another and listened raptly to the statistics: 7 pounds, 9 ounces; 21 inches long; name, David.

Then they showed us the baby, pink and drowsy in his plastic box, and we all beamed fatuously. There were other people there looking through the big glass window at babies. But not, of course, at the right baby—the amazing, astonishing, totally unique baby that was ours.

For some time it has comforted me to notice that in nature death has a certain rhythm: old leaves die and fall from the trees that new ones may come along, and from seemingly dead stalks of chrysanthemums in the garden new chrysanthemums get a start on life. It makes the death of people I love easier to accept.

But to move on and give way to others isn't easy for the young. I have a hard time with it, and I notice that my granddaughter Susy is in active rebellion.

Susy was only five when her cousin David was born. She had been the family's dearly beloved baby all five of those years, and she abhorred and deplored being displaced by a johnny-come-lately.

We thought we had prepared her for the advent of the new baby. She helped us get his room ready. She contributed her old nursery furniture and helped her mother paint it. She even threw in her outgrown baby clothes and a toy or two. But the day the baby made his appearance, no longer a fantasy fellow to be talked about but a yelling, eating, sleeping real live baby, Susy began to take a jaundiced look at the situation.

She was visiting her next-door neighbor Maureen Smith while her mother and I waited at the hospital. When the baby was born, the joyful word was phoned to Maureen's mother with the request that Susy be informed that she had a new cousin. Right away, Pat Smith saw that Susy wasn't overjoyed. When Susy's godmother came to pick her up to take her to supper, Mrs. Smith warned her that Susy might not care for any new-baby congratulations and jubilation.

Anxious to assess the climate early, Susy demanded of her godmother, "Mary, do you like babies?"

"No, I don't!" Mrs. Singleton said promptly. "And I especially don't like boy babies."

Susy relaxed and had a pleasant evening until her mother arrived to take her home. Her mother may have carried on a little, being rather sappy about babies herself, until Susy finally shut her up.

"Let's not talk about you-know-what," she said firmly.

Forewarned, I took Susy with me to visit her new cousin first by sweetening her up with some chocolate-covered cherries and then by telling her that what I had in mind was to let the little newcomer see her, his pretty cousin. It would, I assured her, make him a happy fellow in a strange world.

Susy liked the cherries and she approved of the way the baby looked in her old bed. She even suffered him to lie in her arms for a minute, but she wasn't cooing. She looked him over carefully, handed him back, and picked up a picture book.

When we were leaving, she let me hold her hand a step or two and then she withdrew it.

"All right," she said resignedly. "You want to make some remarks about *him,* don't you?"

"Not me," I said hastily. "What about you? Is there anything you want to say about him?"

"Not a thing," said Susy.

From time to time I hear from my children about the age child I like best. Little babies because you can tuck them in their beds and go dig in the yard. Toddlers because they are responsive; hold out your arms and they run into them. (Sometimes. If you try to take them shopping with you they disappear under dress racks or behind soft-drink displays and you can't find them until you hear a crash.) Teenagers because they can bring in fireplace wood, cut grass, and change tires and will eat absolutely anything you decide to cook.

Some ages are more interesting than others, some more exhausting. Just to look at runabout children makes my back hurt. And then in the cool of the evening take one of that age, all bathed and powdered and ready for bed, out to swing in the hammock under the maple tree, and you forget the spillings and breakings, the chasing and lifting that went on all day. The squeak of the hammock chains, the sleepy sounds of the birds, the gradual onset of darkness suddenly seem endowed with magic. Baby hands that pulled the cat's tail, banged the screen door a thousand times, broke plates, and tipped over flower pots are still and somehow as appealing as starfish or open roses.

All ages have their charm. But there have been times when I was convinced that everybody needs a ten-year-old boy. That's the age, I'm certain, when a boy young'un is more company, more pleasure, and more help than at any other time in his life.

He's old enough to be housebroken, of course, and although he may not be meticulous about bathing and dressing himself, he can sluff off a layer or two of the muck while playing with boats in the bathtub with no bother to anybody else. Who cares if he has cockleburrs in his hair and hasn't combed it since some time last month?

He's also self-reliant about food. If it isn't cooked and set before him, he'll find it and eat it anyhow. He can, if it interests him, even fry up something for himself, usually something Euell Gibbonsish like daylily buds. He certainly isn't bound by Julia Child standards about what is suitable for certain meals. If there's watermelon to be had, it tastes as good to him for breakfast as at any other time.

A ten-year-old boy is old enough to eschew the childish prattle of his earlier years and talk about important things like books and how to make an outrigger boat out of bamboo or did you ever eat alligator eggs?

He's a contemplative being, the ten-year-old boy, who can hang by his knees from the limb of a tree, looking at the world upside down for long moments without breaking the silence of a summer evening. He can sit on his spine with his head tilted back and look at the sky for hours, as quiet as a cattail in a placid pool or a leaf on a windless night.

A ten-year-old boy is a chivalrous fellow, appreciative of his elders and uncritical of his peers. He's patriotic. Unlike his elders, he sees very little that's wrong with his country and a lot that is gloriously right.

He knows the Boy Scout oath, the Pledge of Allegiance to the Flag, and can sing nearly all of the "Star-Spangled Banner," no more off-key than anybody else. His favorite word is "neat," although he isn't, and his only expletive is "Neat-o!"

A ten-year-old boy isn't self-conscious about telling you that he likes you, hugging you hard with skinny all elbows arms or crawling into your bed at night because he's afraid you got cold or lonely. He'll say now what he'll never say later: "You're the best grandma in the whole world."

And when he is driven away from you, he hangs out the back window throwing you kisses with a grubby paw.

At the age of ten a boy is, maybe for the last time in his life, eager to please you, enthusiastic about helping you. Take him on a trip to Disney World, and you don't find out until later that he was too old to ride on the merry-go-round but hid his embarrassment and boarded it anyhow because you were crazy to do it.

Mention to him that you have a burning desire to mulch your flowerbeds with old sawdust and maybe sprinkle a little on your compost pile, and he whirls into action. Older boys would find the sawdust pile troublesome to get to, a snarl of honeysuckle roots and not worth the trouble. A ten-year-old boy finds it a challenge, a gold mine in the jungle, and joyfully figures out a complicated system whereby he can transport the rich dark mulch up the hill to the wheelbarrow, transfer it to the red wagon, and tow it by riding mower to the garden. What does it matter that he makes work for himself, that pushing the wheelbarrow all the way would be easier? He's helping you, isn't he? That's not work but high adventure.

If you have a ten-year-old boy in your family, you'd better hold him close and cherish him. Above all, know what you have—for the age isn't forever.

A few years ago I was amused and a little aghast to read in "Dear Abby" a young wife's complaint that her mother-in-law repeats herself. Sometimes, whined the daughter-in-law, the old girl tells a story from the past that she has already told twenty times. Abby coped with the problem with her usual sensible advice, reminding the young wife that when she reached the age of her mother-in-law she might become a tad repetitious herself.

Of course she will, I thought, and what's so bad about repetition? Some of us tell our old stories over and over again, not because we have forgotten telling them before but because we like to polish and perfect them or, better still, hear them once more ourselves.

Since when do we have to have all fresh original material in a family? One of the primary functions of children is to serve as an audience. If you can't get your family to sit still for your old chestnuts, you are condemned to a life of silence. Friends and acquaintances will say, "Yeah, yeah. You told me that already."

But your loving and durable children won't stop you with a cold reminder that you are being tiresome and repetitious. They'll round up a fresh audience for you. They'll say, "Mother, tell Julia May your story about the Christmas orange."

The chances are Julia May hasn't heard it, and that makes it awfully nice for everybody. You have the fun of telling your story, and your children can listen or not as they please, for of course children have long since perfected the art of tuning you out anyhow.

My grandson Bird has even brought this skill to his television watching. When he was a little boy he got hold of some goggles and blanked out the glass lens with cardboard for wearing when he watched the late late "creature feature." He could leave the sound on but slip the goggles over his eyes to shut out what he didn't want to see.

The picky daughter-in-law, I always thought, could profit by his example. She'd better, because her day of bucking an unresponsive audience is surely on the way.

To a child, of course, sixteen is a milestone. There was the January when my daughter Susan attained that auspicious age. The rain dropped off the trees and whispered in the gutters and made a singing noise as it ran into the sewer under the street outside. And in the house she sat hunched over on the sofa with tears, big fat silver tears pouring from her eyes and running off the end of her freckled nose.

"What's the matter?" I cried, dropping raincoat and umbrella and pocketbook. "Are you hurt?"

She shook her head miserably.

"Are you sick? What's wrong?"

She gulped and brushed her eyes with the back of her hand, making great smears across her face.

"I'll tell you," she said. "I've been sixteen years old for *four* days, and I still haven't got my driver's license!"

I wanted to laugh, but in the face of such calamity I couldn't. I wanted to make soothing noises about oh, well, you've got the rest of your life to drive a car and it's not such a high privilege anyhow.

But that wouldn't do either. When you've been counting the days until your sixteenth birthday for about two years, four extra unallowed-for days of delay amount to a lifetime.

"I'm sorry," I said. "You know how it's been—something every afternoon. I haven't had time to take you to State Patrol headquarters."

She understood that the license bureau's hours were not necessarily going to jibe with my free time but still . . . the tears, the disappointment. So I agreed to let her be late for school and to arrange for myself to be late for work so we could make the momentous journey to the bureau the next morning.

Then I went to bed to pull the covers over my head and try to forget all the new anxiety, all the family squabbles, all the tensions attendant upon having another teen-age driver in the family. But you cry peace, and there is no peace.

She came with that little book the State Department of Public Safety puts out and sat on my feet and asked me questions. How much visibility must a public carrier have before stopping to unload or take on passengers on the highway? How many days do you have to report an accident to the director of public safety? How many feet does it take to stop a vehicle traveling at a speed of thirty miles an hour? (She called it "vee-hickle.")

"Look," I said, "I've got my driver's license. I've been driving by ear since I was fourteen years old—and I can't worry about all that stuff now. It makes my head hurt."

"Mother!" She was shocked. "You mean you don't know the *rules?*"

"Comes the time when I need a rule, I know it," I said with dignity, putting a book up before my face. "I've never had an accident or had to go to traffic court in my life. See if you can do as well."

She finally went to bed, clutching the Safety Department's bible to her heart, and we did get up early and head for the State Patrol headquarters. I stood around with a lot of other mothers, yawning and drinking vend-ing-machine coffee and praying that she would pass. She hooked her loafered feet around the rung of a chair, scratched her head with her pen, and labored over the written test. Then, beaming proudly at a grade of 90, she went off with a trooper for a road test.

When she finally emerged, license in hand, she was smiling radiantly.

"Would you like me to drop you off at the office?" she

asked graciously, beating me to the driver's seat in our car. And then, when we were under way, quite seriously: "Mother, you really ought to study up on the rules. That's one of the dangers on the highway today—middle-aged drivers."

If you have but one car to your name and two teenage drivers in the family, it should come as no surprise to you that you are the public transit system's best customer. Or you walk.

Oddly enough, I found I didn't mind not having the use of my car as much as I minded other parents' knowing about it. There was the night my friend Margaret Long, the novelist, and I were invited out to dinner by a couple who lived off the city bus route. We agreed to go, and then Maggie asked the question I had been skirting. "Can you get your car?"

"Certainly!" I said with that foolhardy positiveness nearly every mother puts on when she knows her ground is shaky. "It's my car, isn't it?"

"Ye-es," she began slowly and then gathered force. "Yes, of course. I could get mine but it's in the shop."

A likely story, I was thinking. Her two teenage daughters probably hadn't let her see the inside of her car since school closed for the summer. If my children were like *that*. . . . I reached for the phone.

Susan answered.

"Honey, I'm going to need the car tonight," I said boldly.

"Hm-m," she said.

"Yes." I went on heartily. "Big evening. Maggie and I are going out to dinner. Need the car."

"Why?" she asked.

"It's a long way out there," I began apologetically. "Some of our pioneer northside friends who live off the trolley line. I need it, I really do."

"What time have you got to be there?" she asked coolly.

I started to tell her but then I stopped myself.

"Why?" I asked cautiously.

"Well, I was thinking we might be able to drop you and pick you up."

"Look," I said desperately. "I've only ridden in the car once this week. I don't mind walking. I'm crazy about riding the bus. But tonight *I need the car!*"

She pulled that ancient trick that mothers used to pull on children. But instead of "Ask your father" it was "Ask your son."

"Like fun I will," I said. "It's my car."

"Yes, ma'am," she said politely. "But he's out in it."

When I caught him he was swamped with errands—all family errands, of course, involving borrowing our hedge clippers back from one neighbor and borrowing another neighbor's edger back from still another neighbor. He had to have the car, he really did.

"Not after seven o'clock," I said. "You won't be working in the yard after seven o'clock, especially if it's raining."

He was silent. Then he said aggrievedly, "How late will you be?"

"Too late for you to use the car," I said daringly. "You'll just have to make other plans."

Another silence fell between us. I could see him going over his list of friends who had the use of automobiles for the evening and recapitulating their plans. I could see the expression on his face—Kit Carson learning that Buffalo Pass was snowed in for the season. It was more of a hardship than one intrepid frontiersman should be called upon to face.

"I'm sorry . . ." I began weakly.

"It's all right," he said gruffly. "I'll manage. But there's the gas situation. It's out."

Sure it's out, I thought. It's always out when I step in the car. "I'll put some in," I offered.

"Oh, in that case . . ." he said, brightening. "I'll leave the keys on your dresser."

I got it, as of course I knew all the time I would. And I showed 'em, all right. I left gas in it too, just like they would have. Twenty-five cents' worth of regular.

Sometimes it seems to me that illness and accidents and growing-up crises are the least of the tribulations of child-rearing. You can cope with exigency. What I have found less tolerable is the continual, unending *talk* of the young. Of course they reach an age where they barely speak to you beyond grunts and monosyllables. But at some stages in their lives they *talk*. Incessantly.

For years I told my family and friends that the thing I abhorred the most in the world was conversation after midnight.

Talk to me early, I pleaded. Let's solve the problems of this world when the night is young. Let's exchange confidences before our minds and eyes are befogged with sleep.

So what did they do? Every single soul to whom I am related by blood or marriage turned out to be the kind of person who never gets in top conversational form until midnight.

I recall one particular example. It was a night when I had a good book to read, when the rain fell softly outside, and except for routine family noises the household seemed settled. Of course our routine family noises would have sounded like bedlam in some dwelling places. Time and custom had muted them for me. I could hear the record player in the girls' room braying "Young Love," eggs frying in the kitchen for a midnight snack, and my son alternately listening to and trying to imitate the trombonist Jack Teagarden in the next room, without really hearing anything. Those noises, being usual and more or less constant, were like the soughing of the wind in a peaceful pine glade to me.

So I read a little, listened to the rain, and thought about what spring might be doing to the mountain slopes in north Georgia where we had a weekend shack. Then comes Mary, age fourteen, with a fried egg and peanut butter sandwich and a great gnawing hunger for talk.

There was no place in the house so well adapted to eating as my bed, so naturally she crawled up and sat on my feet.

"Is he going in the army?" she said, nodding toward her brother's room.

"Oh, sometime," I said lightly. And then more firmly. "But not tonight. He's going to bed in a few minutes, I hope. As soon as he perfects the chromatic scale. And you'd better put up that gook and go to bed too."

"Oh, I hope he won't!" she said tragically, eating the gook. "The world's in such a terrible state . . . there's sure to be a war."

"Now, now," I began soothingly.

"There *is*, Mother!" she said around the fried egg and peanut butter. "Egypt and Russia and all. You don't know. You always wanta look on the bright side."

"That's right," I said. "I'm an optimist. I keep hoping everybody will go to bed so they won't be late for school in the morning."

"Mother!" she said reproachfully. "You don't pay a bit of attention to the inner-national situation. Can't you tell the world is bad off? We've gone about as far as we can go, and the next war will be the end of the world."

Suddenly I became conscious of the other noises: a callow teenage-idol type braying "Young Love" in one part of the house and the mournful notes of "Abide with Me" from a trombone in another. "Abide with me, fast falls the eventide," went the old funeral hymn. Eventide had fallen, and I was certainly being abided with.

"Excuse me," I said, trying to dislodge her from my feet. "I think I might as well get up and wash the dishes I stacked to wash in the morning."

"Good!" she said. "I'll come and sit and talk to you. Do you know that ten years from now everything's going to be so awful you and I might be trying to kill each other for more food?"

I *hate* conversation after midnight!

The penchant for talk is not confined to one generation, of course. Susy, my granddaughter, has it. At almost five years Susy explained my duty as a grandmother to me. I was to teach her things, she said. Fine, I said, around a mouthful of hairpins which I was using to hitch up the tide of auburn hair that keeps falling in Susy's eyes. What did she want to know?

What, she inquired, is an institution?

Has anybody else tried to explain institutions around a mouthful of pins to a five-year-old? That was the beginning of a long day. We had many things to do, and Susy had a million questions about them. There was the old slop jar I bought at a house sale. I had in mind filling it with Queen Anne's lace and pink roses.

"What's a slop jar?" asked Susy.

Her older brothers chimed in. "Yeah, what's a slop jar?"

Pointing to the new acquisition was not enough. I had to wax eloquent about the fine china amenities that preceded indoor plumbing. They were convulsed. They looked at my jar with its pretty raised flowers on the side and its bail and said, "Ugh! Gross!"

We walked to the mailbox to post a birthday card Susy had for her cousin Sibley. And that brought on a full-scale inquiry into the duties and methods of the postal service. The ceremony of raising the red flag to notify the rural carrier that mail waited within the box intrigued her. She had never before realized that the stamps affixed to the outside of an envelope paid for this service, and she was fascinated that a stamp would buy someone in a right-hand-drive jeep who would come all the way from the post office ten miles away and pick up a birthday card and get it all the way to New Orleans or Texas or Indiana for a little girl.

With that settled we went home to make ice cream, and the freezer was a wonder to Susy. We went for a swim in the lake, and by that time I was talked out. But Susy had a new and far more unsettling topic.

She was kiting over the grass in her thin little nightgown, her hair still damp.

"I think I want to go home to my mama," she remarked.

"Ah, no," I said, pinning bathing suits and towels to the line. "You're here to spend the night with me. We're going to have fun. Soon as I get through here I'll get you some cookies and ice cream."

She looked thoughtful, unconvinced, ready to go either way.

"My mama has taught me a lot of things," she said, leading the way to the back porch and the ice cream. "Do you know copperheads are so poison if you don't get help right away they can kill you and you'll die? Really die?"

"Hm-m," I said.

"And my mama knows about rattlesnakes," she said, getting in the big rocker and grasping her ankles in her hands so that by tilting her little body she could make it rock.

"Hm-m," I said again, thinking to myself that her mama is sure full of bad news. "What else did your mama teach you?"

"She taught me how to hang from my knees," she said with a sudden whoop, tipping herself upside down and hooking her knees over the back of the rocker.

I set her bowl of ice cream on the table out of range of her heels and found myself a chair. The crisis hadn't shaped up, I decided. She was going to be content to spend the night. Her mother hadn't been feeling well, and I thought by bringing the children to the country she might get some rest. The boys, upstairs watching television, would be no problem. But a soon-to-be five-year-old might miss her mama in the night, and the last thing I wanted at bedtime was tears and/or a trip back to Atlanta.

The rocking chair was squeaking, and she wanted to play the "What did it say?" game. I was tired. It had been a long day, and I thought despairingly that if squeaking rockers took up conversation I was done for.

"Listen to the birds," I suggested, knowing they at least would shut up when it got dark. "Come sit in my lap and see if you can tell what they're saying."

The dusk was heavy with heat, but presently a little breeze ruffled the peach trees and set a hanging basket to swaying lightly. Birds chattered sleepily in the old cherry tree back of the garden. Her small face with its bright brown eyes and frame of dark-red pond-damp hair was still with listening.

"I hear the mama bird," she whispered. "She is telling the children birds it's bedtime."

I listened and heard it too. "Sleep, sleep!" she was saying peremptorily.

"And the children birds are saying they are hungry. And the daddy bird . . . ?"

"He's saying, 'Hush your mouth and go to sleep, I hauled you plenty of worms today!' " I summed up from my vast experience.

She giggled. "Do birds really talk like that?"

Um-m, I wondered. Maybe all parents talk like that. They get tired and don't want to sit around in the heat and gathering darkness and listen to a lot of chatter. They want to rest their wings and their claws from flying and scratching and have a little quiet.

"Sleep, sleep!" I echoed the bird.

She nodded and collected three dolls and a red calico elephant and followed me into the house and to the bedroom. Moments later I moved a rubber doll leaking bath water to a windowsill and smoothed Susy's nightie over her knees and turned the electric fan to its slowest speed.

Her long auburn lashes curled on her rosy cheeks, and she sighed in her sleep.

For a moment there, standing beside her, I wondered why I had put her to bed so early.

Sometimes a mother gets tired, and if there is anything more exhausting than exhaustion it is having children to help you rest. My own were teenagers, and I came home from the office after a long day, wanting nothing so much as bed. They had had their dinner, and mine was all ready. I was to take a hot bath, climb right into bed, and they would bring me a tray. You don't really need a tray for a hot dog, but they fixed one anyhow, with a flower on it in a teetering bud vase and a cup of very strong coffee—to keep me awake while I was resting.

Any woman who has had children as long as she can remember knows rest in the midst of the family is not pure and unadulterated. You have to put a hem in an urgently needed dress, eat soupy custard they saved for you, listen to a new Elvis Presley record, and talk to somebody's mother over the phone about a birthday party. All this before the ritual known as Rolling Up My Hair begins.

It seems to me that girls don't roll up their hair nowadays, and I count that progress for the human race. When my daughters did it, it was just the prelude to an interminable period of loving, ceremonious attention to the whole body and minute searching of the soul.

Questions like "Mother, do you think I ought to paint my toenails?" and solemn paeans beginning "I *wish* I knew what to do about my duck!" (a hairstyle, not a barnyard fowl) were easy to ignore. I could even listen to them puffing and blowing and beating their bottoms on the floor in an effort to look trim in the new-style pants. But then the Serious Talk starts.

"At last, Mother, I know your secret," was the way Mary began it.

"What secret?" I asked casually. Not that I had one, but you never know.

"I'm adopted," she said.

"Pooh," I scoffed, trying to wiggle the foot she was sitting on. "Get off my feet and go to bed."

"No, really, Celestine," she said, "it's time we were realistic about this."

"You call me 'Mother'!" I said automatically.

"If you insist," she said with an indulgent air. "But I know the truth. You and Daddy—I mean your husband, Jim—you all adopted me from a famous Hollywood producer. My true mother was a famous actress. You were sweet to take me in, but now I know."

"Ha," I said morosely. "Pure soap opera. You stop watching that stuff."

She was examining herself in the mirror on the closet door, raising first one eyebrow and then the other, sucking in her cheeks to make Katharine Hepburn hollows and letting a look of haughty langour half close her brown eyes.

"Just look at me," she said. "All your other children are redheaded. I always did think it was tacky," she mused, watching her sister coping with the bright red ends of the unhappy "duck." "Now I'm glad to know that I'm not a bit of kin to any of you."

She smoothed her hair and widened her eyes.

"My poor famous actress mother died before I was . . . I

mean *when* I was born. And here I am with you people."
She sighed. "It explains why you have never really loved
me."

"Now look here," I said, sitting up in bed so fast the
hot-dog tray, my own supply of murder mysteries, boxes
of bobby pins, and unfinished sewing tumbled to the floor.
"I'm tired of this lousy joke."

"Really, Celestine," she interrupted, giggling. "Do let
us be realistic about this."

From her position on the floor, her sister settled the matter for both of us with the classic line from *Born Yesterday*.

"Leave us," she said languidly, "not conduct ourselves
like a slob."

It was no way to spend a restful evening at home.

Boy children, I find, are not given to talk on the scale that
girl young'uns are. It may have something to do with all
that hair rolling up. As a young man I know once pointed
out, "A bobby-pinny session has to be dialoguey." No
child, of course, tells you everything, but who says you
need to know everything?

When Jimmy was fourteen his sisters were down in
Florida visiting their grandmother and I was congratulat-
ing myself on a peaceful, one-child summer. He had his
own interests, his own private pursuits, and he could take
a mother or leave her alone, giving the edge, I sometimes
thought, to leaving her alone. Clothes didn't worry him,
so there was none of that preoccupation with ironing ruf-
fles and digging up hair ribbons. He would settle for jeans
and a T-shirt, clean or dirty.

Food was no trouble, just as long as it was where he
could find it. He could eat hamburgers three times a day

and was amiable about fixing them himself. Confidences and conversations with me didn't interest him. He usually had good friends sprawled out in his room waiting to help him settle some pressing problem, such as, Is Hitler really dead or is he flourishing in a hideaway in Little America like it says in the *Police Gazette?*

He never telephoned to say plaintively, "Mother, what can I *do-o?*" because he was afraid I'd think of something.

So it seemed to me that I was in for a restful month or two. At least that's what I kept telling everybody. Then I went home and he greeted me from the living-room rug where he was surrounded by eight volumes from the encyclopedia, looking gratifyingly studious.

"Mama, don't go in the kitchen," he said.

"Why not?"

"It might blow up," he explained casually.

"Blow up!" I yelped. "What are you talking about?"

"Well, I made me a still," he said. "Just like a whiskey still, only I haven't got any whiskey yet. I'm just working with water in the experimental stage. But I'm not sure it won't blow up."

I galloped to the kitchen, and he followed me at a distance. There on the stove was an old coffee can boiling away at a great rate, and from it ran a Rube Goldberg–looking aluminum coil, patched here and there with black friction tape. At the end of the coil was a teacup, catching an occasional clear drop.

"You see, Mama, it's distilled water," he said proudly. "Would you like to try some?"

I backed away and he followed me, explaining enthusiastically how he had made himself a "worm" and had a funnel all set to catch the product of his still. He had learned all about it from the encyclopedia. The only trouble was that water was a little tame to work with. Did I think we could afford a bottle of wine so he could make us some first-rate brandy?

"Brandy?" I said dazedly.

"Yes'm," he said. "You never know when somebody will faint around here, and what would you do? You always have to have brandy when somebody faints."

I started to say that I had never fainted in my life, but I looked at the contraption on the middle of my kitchen stove and reconsidered. That could have been the summer I took to fainting.

Although my children, since they grew up, sometimes compliment me by telling their children that they were "rich kids" when they were young, it certainly wasn't money-rich. They had many things, the least of which was cold cash, and looking back, I suppose that was good. I don't think perhaps a little more money would have been corrupting. Still, you don't know what it could have led to.

Take the time Jimmy went forth with his friend Bill to spend the $2.00 his aunt stuck in a letter to him.

"Me and Bill want to go to town," he said.

"All right, but it's 'Bill and I,'" I said, "and don't be late for supper."

They weren't late for supper, and I didn't think to inquire into their shopping expedition for a while—until, that is, he said casually, "Mama, how come tattooing is so expensive?"

"Is it?" I asked absently.

"Boy!" he said. "You can't hardly get anything for less than five or ten dollars."

"You can't?" I murmured. "How do you know?"

"Well, me and Bill—I mean, Bill and I—we went to that tattoo shop and I just wanted something simple—you know, a snake or a rose or a little flag or something. And do you know, even with my two dollars, there wasn't a thing I could get!"

"You mean," I said, finally grasping the situation, "you were going to be *tattooed?*"

"Sure," he said. "I didn't have money enough to help out much in buying a Model-T and I thought I might as well. Lots of sailors do. Daddy knew a man one time that had a three-masted schooner under full sail on his chest. 'Course I knew I couldn't afford *that.*"

" 'Course," I echoed stupidly.

"But Bill had a lot of money and he was real interested in getting something kind of . . . well, you know, snazzy. We asked the man if it hurt, and he just laughed and said, 'I refer that question to this lady here.' There was a lady selling jewelry in there, so we asked her if it hurt to be tattooed and she laughed and said no, it didn't. She said she had been tattooed hundreds of times and she was tender-skinned too and she could hardly feel it at all."

"And tender-skinned, too," I croaked.

"Yes'm," he said. "But when we asked about a tattoo with poetry and roses and maybe a flag waving, we found out you couldn't get anything we could afford."

"Thank the Lord," I breathed fervently.

"We gonna have to save up," he said.

"Have you got your two dollars?" I asked craftily, seized by an impulse to filch it.

"Oh, no'm," he said. "We got some hamburgers and milkshakes and our money is gone. We had to walk home, and now I'm hungry again. Is supper ready?"

The buying of a dress for Susan's first piano recital was one of those unexpected expenses. I had known about the recital for months, had even gone along with her to pick out John Jacob Niles's lovely Christmas folk song, "Jesus, Jesus Rest Your Head" for the holiday program. But, as usual, I hadn't given any thought to what she would wear.

Suddenly it was upon me. Not just a dress but a *long* dress!

"A formal," Susan specified.

We all looked at her, gulping a little. Eleven years old and a formal. Gracious.

"You could make it, Mother," she suggested tentatively. "Maybe you could cut down something or do something over."

But her heart wasn't in the suggestion and I knew it. Of course, I was an older woman when I got my first important gown of that kind—an older woman of sixteen—but it had not been a real success because it was one of those cut-down, made-over, hand-me-down jobs. No, it would have to be a boughten dress if we ate black-eyed peas for a month.

So the whole family embarked on the shopping expedition. With his hands jammed down in his pea jacket pockets and his stocking cap on the back of his head, Jimmy looked like a lanky and uneasy dockhand in the mirrored and carpeted department store. And Mary, sticking out a dingy little hand to finger net and lace and velvet, withdrew the paw without making contact, she was that awed.

Susan bustled ahead giving out voluble orders. She was not going to be hampered, interfered with, or advised by (1) a derisive older brother or (2) a nosy little sister.

Then we hit the department of dresses for chubby little girls edging into their teens, and everything was quiet. There were so many of them, all rich lustrous materials and lovely colors, and they seemed so foreign to our world of blue jeans and gingham school dresses whipped up by a thrifty grandmother.

She stood before a row in a glass case, not daring to touch anything, until a saleswoman came to help us. When she came she seemed easy with the task and selected an armload of dresses and led Susan off into a fitting room.

Presently my child came back. She was still a plump little sixth-grader, and her scuffed loafers and socks showed plainly beneath the ballerina-length skirt. And yet in the full silken dress of green there was something about her—a quality of quietness, of grace.

"Oh, Susan," breathed Mary.

"Gee," said Jimmy.

I said nothing, but Susan caught my eye in the mirror and I knew this had to be the dress. She smoothed the bodice and tilted her head to admire the effect. Then she gave the dress her seal, the final seal of approval.

"Can I have it, Mother? It . . . it makes me look so *old*."

Having them grow up is a mixed blessing for a parent and, I suppose, the same for the child. Mary was also eleven when she realized life was passing her by.

I found her standing by the window looking out on the gray winter sky with the branches of the sweet-gum tree as bare as picked bones. There was a melancholy droop to her shoulders, and she brushed her bangs out of her eyes and sighed tragically.

"What's the matter?" I asked.

"It's just life," she said, sighing again. "You know I just realized I've wasted my childhood."

"Eleven isn't so old," I offered. "You've got a few more years."

She shook her head dolefully. "Just a year, I figure. One more year of childhood—that's all."

She turned from the window, sat down heavily, and began to count off the rosary of lost opportunities, beginning with the tricycle age and coming up to her elderly present. She mourned the books she hadn't read, the playhouses she hadn't built, the mud pies she hadn't made.

There wasn't much I could say to cheer her, because suddenly I felt sad myself.

Fortunately, the invitation to the sixth-grade square dance came and she was diverted. Between brushing her hair, borrowing her sister's crinoline petticoat, and subduing the bright flash of lipstick to a point where we'd let her out of the house, she was too busy to worry about her misspent youth. And after she was gone I was so busy worrying about whether she would have a good time I forgot the mud pies and tricycles.

When she came in, her new age surrounded her like an aura.

"Mother, I had the bes-st time!" she said breathlessly.

"There were just plenty of boys at the dance, and we had so much fun!"

As she undressed she told me every lovely detail, and when she finally climbed into bed she said dreamily, "You know, I believe I'm going to like being grown."

In the midst of my relief I noticed a small quiet ache in my heart when I turned out the light. An eleven-year-old should be eager to grow up. Growing and looking ahead and enjoying today is so much healthier than all that repining for days long gone. But she was my youngest—the baby. I tried to visualize what it would be like to have them not only grown but gone from the house, and I went to sleep feeling very sorry for myself.

The next day I heard a mighty racket in the back yard and groped my way to the window, still caught up in the mood of the night before. Children were playing in the back yard, but not my children. My children were growing up.

Then I heard her voice and saw her leap through the air. She had a tree branch for a gun and she was aiming surely at the heart of the nine-year-old in the cowboy suit and screeching, "*A-a-a-at!* I gotcha! You're dead!"

There was mud on her knees and a scratch on her cheek and not the sign of a flouncy petticoat, a lipstick, or a grown-girlish air. Suddenly I felt better—but confused. Could it be there's a time when a child is both a little girl and a woman and all the ages at once?

I f it hadn't been for the children I would never have
acquired a shack in the north Georgia mountains.
Their father had died and it was not the kind of place
for a woman alone, being primitive and remote. But the
children loved what they had seen of the mountains, and
I thought they needed mountain experience. So once on a
story in the hill country I said to our Ellijay friend and the
paper's correspondent, Herbert Tabor, "If you ever find a
place I could buy, will you please let me know?"

A few days later, Mr. Tabor called me. "I've found two
places," he said. "One is a five-room house with eight
acres of land and a creek for twenty-five hundred dollars.
The other is a two-room shack on one acre of land with a
creek for five hundred."

"Show me the five-hundred-dollar one," I said promptly.

The very next Sunday, a chilly gray day in November,
we packed a picnic lunch, and the children and Muv and
I drove up to see the cabin. It was indeed a shack. Some
men from Ellijay had thrown together two rooms and a
little half-screen, half-boarded-up porch for shelter in deer-
hunting and rainbow-trout seasons. It contained a rough
deal table, some shelves, and a wood stove in the kitchen
and a couple of saggy beds and a heater in the bigger

room. Everything was overlaid with a patina of dirt, rat leavings, and dried leaves that had blown in through the cracks.

There was a privy in the back yard, a creek in the front yard, and, for drinking water, a spring across the footlog and up the gravel road a piece.

It was, the children and I decided, the most beautiful place in the world!

Muv was skeptical. A hundred miles from Atlanta, she pointed out, in the wilderness (her name for the Chatta-hoochee National Forest), with no electricity, no plumb-ing, no telephone, and the only neighbor a man with a similar shack a little way up the creek who usually came only in sourwood season, bringing a dozen hives of bees with him. What did we want with it?

We wanted all that, we told her, and the rest.

We wanted a mountain that rose gently behind the cabin, climbing eventually to the beautiful blue 'Tater Patch summit where, back in the 1930s, the CCC boys had built the lovely little Lake Conasauga, now a state park with swimming dock and picnic areas. We wanted Holly Creek itself, a silver stream that rushed over rocks, falling into crystal pools, swirling around banks of rhodo-dendron, mountain laurel, and ferns, making the loveliest music we had ever heard right there in the front yard. We wanted the forest of hemlock and hardwood trees which framed and encompassed the little house with color even on that gray day, pulsing and burning in a conflagra-tion of beauty.

"Mama, can we have it?" asked Jimmy, Susan, and Mary.

Busy building a fire in the kitchen stove and hauling

water from the spring to fill the old kettle the hunters had left behind, I made tea and helped Muv spread the picnic lunch on the little porch before I answered.

It seemed to me tea made with that spring water on that wood stove was the most delicious I ever drank. And it seemed that I was drinking it in the most enchanting place in the world.

I turned to Mr. Tabor and said, "How much would we have to pay down?"

"How much can you pay down?" he countered.

At that point in our lives there was no money for nonessentials. We had acquired the services of an accountant friend, John Cook, as a business manager. He had looked over my finances and taken money management out of my hands. I deposited my pay, he wrote the checks for the bills, and we had an allowance which had absolutely no stretch. It was a wonderful service he performed—not for pay, as he explained to me in the beginning, but because it was such a challenge. The children were getting what they needed: braces for teeth, shoes and soup and music lessons. We even had the first new kitchen stove in family history and the first new car. But there wasn't going to be enough money passing through my hands to buy a second home. I wouldn't even mention it to Mr. Cook.

To Mr. Tabor I said, "We want it. Don't sell it to anybody else. Let me see what I can do."

A few days later the program chairman for a Rotary Club ladies' night sent me a check for $75 for a speech I had made. Jubilant, I told the children but not Mr. Cook.

What should I do with it?

"Buy Holly Creek!" they chorused.

And we did. Mr. Tabor persuaded the hunters to take $75 down and $25 a month. I gave up lunches and walked to work to save bus fare. The children gave up Saturday movies and sessions at the dime store. We salvaged the $25 a month out of our allowance, and we spent every weekend we could at Holly Creek.

For them it was an opportunity to learn first-hand how their ancestors had lived. They chopped and hauled wood for heat, filled and cleaned kerosene lamps for light, and brought dripping buckets of water from the spring for cooking and dishwashing. In summer they bathed in the icy waters of the creek. In winter they found a dishpan full of water heated on the kitchen stove was adequate to their needs. (I think of that often nowadays when I see Jacuzzis whirling in new houses and read magazine pieces about "sensual" bathrooms.)

The outhouse set in the bushes up the hill with its back to us was the hardest thing to accept, but they came around eventually. Learning from Mr. Tabor that it was a WPA pit privy, apparently the Cadillac of privies, impressed them. Then Jimmy noted that the outhouse roof was an old tin Woco-Pep gasoline sign and that Woco-Pep signs, long since gone from the motoring scene, were collector's items. Our privy's value and distinction were secure.

Still we sang and beat on tin pans as we approached it, hoping to frighten away any snakes it might harbor. And I noticed that the city tendency to monopolize the bathroom did not prevail where the privy was concerned. People went in desperation and returned with alacrity. Except my friend Margaret Long.

Maggie and her daughters went often to the cabin with

us, and I remember one special occasion watching her prepare for a trip to the privy. It was raining and cold, and she first put on galoshes; then she buttoned herself into a coat. She topped this costume with a knitted cap. Then she looked around and collected her cigarettes and the book she was reading.

As she got outside she turned and held up the book.

"I won't finish it this time," she said.

The book's title: *War and Peace.*

Gradually we fixed the cabin a little. The Tabors gave us a big wood range, retired from their kitchen, and we installed it in one corner of the bigger room, which we decided to make a living room–kitchen. I bought an old sink at the Salvation Army store and Mr. Tabor set it near the stove, putting in windows above it and a cabinet beneath. Water did not run into the cabin, but it was a surprising convenience to have it run out when Mr. Tabor connected a piece of plastic pipe to the sink and had it drain under a rock in the back yard. A Stone Mountain friend gave us a big metal icebox. We bought a wicker settee at the Goodwill for $7, and a carpenter came out from Ellijay and constructed a pair of boxes which, with mattresses on them, served as beds at night and lounges in the daytime. We extended and fully screened the porch overlooking the creek. What had been the kitchen became a little bedroom, and one Christmas the children pooled their resources and bought me one of the most magnificent presents I ever received: a Franklin stove, which heated the room as the old wood stove had done and warmed and brightened our spirits as well, with its open fire.

In the living room an old mountain chimney mason

built us a fireplace from rocks hauled one Saturday by convict crews under the direction of our friend the county commissioner. I didn't realize until later that this was probably an illegal transaction. The commissioner, Joshua Logan, called "Jedge" Logan from his days as a justice of the peace, told us that the convicts were entitled to have Saturday afternoon off from public works but that they liked to make a little spending money when they could. I could pay them; and the county, abounding in rocks, would spare me some for them to haul.

It was my daughters' idea that we should have a hot lunch for them, so with the help of the Tabors, who arrived with viands from their kitchen, we spread a lavish meal on the old deal table and sat down to lunch with Judge Logan, the chimney mason, and half a dozen men and boys wearing the blue-striped uniforms of the Georgia prisoners. My children never forgot, as they sat before their bright hearth fire on a winter night, that we were indebted in a measure to men who were in trouble, men who were not free, for warmth and comfort.

Months later a reporter from our paper was engaged in writing an exposé of county commissioners who used convict labor on private property. I was in south Georgia covering a rose festival when I walked into the hotel dining room for breakfast and saw the headline. Commissioner Joshua Logan of Gilmer County had erred in this matter. He had put convicts to work on private property!

I neglected my toast and coffee and devoured the story. My chimney and I weren't mentioned, but I had to call my boss and confess.

"Convicts hauled rocks for my chimney at Holly Creek," I stammered guiltily when I got the managing editor on the line. "I paid them, but—"

"You paid them?" William Fields, my boss, asked. "How much?"

I told him.

"Well, you probably won't be indicted since you paid them," Fields grumbled, "but you know that's a form of graft and utterly reprehensible." He softened a bit. "There's always this: The kind of graft you received nobody else would have."

It's not true today, of course. City home builders would pay a pretty penny for those rocks, which were so numerous after the chimney was finished it took us months to get them out of the yard. The children and I spent many weekend hours hauling them to the edge of the yard and stacking them in what turned out to be a pretty little wall along the road which crossed our creek and led to the beekeeper's cabin.

Judge Logan became one of our most welcome friends and visitors. He would arrive with the Tabors on a Sunday afternoon and sit awhile in the yard by the creek and tell us of old days in the mountains where he was born and raised. Most mountain people were very poor then, and young Joshua counted himself lucky to get a job working for the railroad one year. He was a small boy and barefoot, and he labored to cut crossties and haul them, one at a time, with a little bull yearling calf.

It was slow and arduous work, but he got 25 cents a tie, he told the children.

"Most money I ever made," he said.

"What did you do with it, Judge?" Jimmy asked.

The judge chuckled.

"Bought myself the finest thing I ever owned: a pair of

copper-toed shoes. Not homemade of stiff cowhide tanned by my papa, mind you, but store-bought. Copper-toed!"

It was a lesson in appreciation for my young'uns and may have helped them to remember not to take life's necessaries for granted.

Judge Logan loved the mountains even more ardently than we did. Once, he told us, his father had heard stories of the rich, level farmland in south Georgia and had been seduced into pulling up stakes and setting out for that easeful country. He packed up their house plunder, tied the milk cow to the back of the wagon, called their old hound dog, and headed south.

"It was good land, all right," Judge Logan recalled. "Flat and easy to plow. Not rocky or hilly. But it was boresome to us young'uns, and hot. Mosquitoes come out of the swamps and gnawed on us. We come down with the malaria fever. The well water was warmish and flat tasting, like the land."

One morning, Judge Logan reported, they were awakened by the mournful howling of their old hound. He sat in the yard and lifted his muzzle and poured out his sorrow in a quivering ululation of sadness.

"Papa went to the door and looked out and saw him," Judge Logan related. "'That does it,' he said. And he turned to us and said, 'Young'uns, load the wagon. We're going back to the mountains. I say damn a place even a dog can't stand!'"

Our dog Abel was also a mountain lover. Properly named Judge Abel Sinclair for a character in the unpublished novel of our doctor and friend, William R. Crowe, who gave him to us, Abel was the most durable and memorable of a long chain of dogs in our family. He was a big, squarish, smelly cocker spaniel with a nose which Dr. Crowe, a cocker fancier, considered too long for his breeding. (This was a judgment which incensed my children, who considered that snub-nosed cockers suffered by comparison.) He went everywhere with us—some places by family agreement and planning, the rest because the children smuggled him along. I remember one night when we attempted to sneak off to the neighborhood movie, Abel lifted the latch on the screened door and followed us. I took him back once, scolding and berating him every step of the way. We progressed one more block toward the movie, and he caught up with us a second time. I ordered him home, and the children struck.

It came out that I was a selfish, unfeeling wretch to go off to enjoy an evening without Abel, who dearly loved us, wanted to be with us, and was crazy about movies. So we went back home, got the car, and went to a drive-in, where Abel took one look at Joseph Cotten and went to sleep.

Of course it was unthinkable to go to Holly Creek without Abel, who took every walk with us, swam beside us, and even leaped up in the hammock to swing with us.

But it wasn't always easy. The April Abel came home from the hospital, where he had been under treatment for a sprained shoulder, I considered leaving him in town. The children wouldn't have it. So we took him along. I remember standing on the footlog and thinking that the creek looked like quicksilver in the moonlight. The tree branches made delicate shadows right down to the edge of the beautiful little stream, and then the water, buxom and bouncy from the spring rains, whipped everything into a froth.

"We've never been up here when the moon wasn't shining," I observed to the children, who were ready to take a walk.

"Mother," said my most realistic child, Susan, "you've got to where you tell the biggest whoppers about Holly Creek. You know you've been up here when it was cold or raining or just pitch-black dark."

I sighed one of my how-sharper-than-a-serpent's-tooth sighs and left the bridge. Of course she was right. I had been to Holly Creek when it was sleeting. (Such lovely pearl-like globules of ice!) I even remembered rainy nights. (Wonderful nights when the rain against the tin roof sounded like a symphony.)

And still . . . it did seem to me that the moon was always shining. Or the sun, as the case might be. Everybody needs a place that's pure magic to them, and Holly Creek was mine. It was my theory that sleep was sweeter; food, even canned beans, tasted better; coffee made with spring water was fit for the gods; and the children, my fractious, ornery, cantankerous young'uns, behaved like cherubim and seraphim under the spell of the mountains and the creek's sweet song.

But I was hard-pressed to preserve that notion on this particular visit. Abel insisted on taking all our walks with us. He started, and then he began limping painfully and was dropping behind. Maggie's daughter Sissy, now a Florida newspaperwoman, had come along for the weekend. She had been cheerful about riding in the car with Abel's feet in her lap and his tail in her face, but she emphatically saw no reason why we should take a walk if we had to carry a fifty-pound cocker spaniel in our arms.

"Well, Sissy," cried one of her little hostesses, "are *you* just home from the hospital? Have *you* had needles stuck in you? Do *your* paws hurt?"

Sissy subsided and took her turn at hefting Abel up and down rocky mountain paths. It slowed up walks, I admit, but they were still lovely.

Holly Creek was the testing ground for friends. It exposed strengths and weaknesses. My friend Margaret Bridges, a doctor's wife conditioned to comfort, took to the primitive state with enthusiasm. I have a mental picture of her squatting on a rock in the middle of the creek admiring the trees, the sky, and the hills as she scrubbed a skillet.

"This is the way people should wash dishes—and clothes," she said. "Beat 'em on a rock. When you go indoors and use gadgets and appliances you take all the fun out of the job."

One studious young girl, who usually spent her time at the creek sitting under a tree reading poetry, was greatly admired by my daughters as an intellectual. (She made all A's, too.) They found that intellectuals, so-called, haven't a cerebral grasp of some things. There was the time she volunteered to help us paint. She painted her end of the wall thoroughly, including everything which hung on it: flyswatter, calendar, somebody's old cap. Then she tackled the floor, and we discovered her slumped miserably in a corner. She had painted herself into it.

It wasn't my idea to break up Susan's romance with a Georgia Tech sophomore when she was sixteen years old. He was, on the whole, the kind of boy mothers cherish. He asked her to dances well ahead of time, he had the use of a car which was years better looking and safer than most which came to our house, and he was very pleasant and mannerly to grown-ups, an admirable quality in the young.

For some reason, Jimmy and his friends couldn't stand him. We invited him to Holly Creek, and I understood why.

The rule there was that the girls slept in the little bedroom, the boys on the big screened porch, and the grown-ups on the box beds in the living room. He had to drag his bed into the living room where I slept because the air on the porch was detrimental to his asthma. He needed a different pillow, he wanted better cover. When the fire burned low he did not replenish it. When wood needed chopping he couldn't be found. He hauled no water from the spring. He refused to join us in a swim because the creek was too cold. And at twilight when he might have presumably enjoyed hammock time with his girl, he complained there were bugs flying around.

When we got back to the city he called and came around a few times, but he got a cool reception from Susan and worse from her brother and his friends. They were scrubbing the front porch and joyfully turning the hose on one another when Susan's erstwhile suitor approached. They turned the hose on him.

We never saw him again.

Fortunately for us, Edward, another Tech boy, passed the Holly Creek test. He liked the little cabin. The hills and the woods and the creek agreed with him so well that he concurred when they were married and Susan wanted to go there on their honeymoon.

And of course Muv's opposition to the place was short-lived. As soon as we got the wood stove and icebox and what she called a "night jar" for the bedroom, she decided that we had amenities enough and became a Holly Creek enthusiast. She arrived with a big pot and put on a hen to cook for chicken and dumplings. The three-legged iron spider with a lid to hold coals, which somebody had given me, was no quaint antique to her but a very practical way of cooking corn bread on the hearth.

We had wonderful fires, and Muv loved to sit before them and recount stories of her childhood on a farm in south Georgia.

"My, that's a good ironing fire," she would remark as the rosy oak coals stirred and sighed in the rock fireplace. "I remember at Grandma's . . ."

And she would be off on a reminiscence about the sad irons lined up before the coals, the starched and ironed meeting shirts of the men and boys in the family, the cooking and yard-sweeping and scrubbing that went on in preparation for the Sabbath.

Sometimes, when I had to be out of town, Muv would come up from Florida to stay with the children, and they would promptly load the car and head for Holly Creek.

Jimmy and his friends sometimes went to the cabin for a weekend when the rest of the family could not go. One memorable autumn they went up just as the deer-hunting season opened. A boy named Jody, who came from a gun-owning family, brought along a proper deer rifle, but Mr. Tabor, who had seen the hazards of the season's opening in the mountains, persuaded the boys to stay close to the cabin and not risk becoming targets in the woods.

"Fool hunters will shoot anything that moves," muttered Mr. Tabor. "Last year they got a farmer's cow. This year, if he's not careful, they'll get his oldest boy."

It was a disappointment to Jody particularly. He liked guns and had counted on using his. He finally did.

Jimmy explained to me when they got home.

"We may have to burn the cabin down to get rid of it," he remarked for openers.

"Get rid of what?" I asked.

"The smell," he said.

The way it happened, he said, they had gone to bed and he was asleep, dreaming he was listening to his favorite band, Benny Goodman. He heard Gene Krupa on the drums and suddenly the tintinnabulation was thunderous. He awakened to find Jody standing over him with a smoking rifle.

"There was a skunk on the kitchen table," Jimmy related. "Jody heard him and got his rifle. He shot the skunk, all right, but the skunk fired first!"

The boys grabbed their blankets and fled to the yard to build a fire and sleep on the ground the rest of the night. Strangely enough, we did not have to do anything drastic to get rid of the skunk smell. Lye water and time took care of it.

Although our enthusiasm for Holly Creek never waned our times there dwindled as the children reached the age where it's death to be separated from the telephone. My friends and I continued to go to the cabin for a time and all of us made an occasional day-long visit to it, picnicking in the yard, after vandals broke in and stole everything in the way of furnishings, including the skillet and the coffee pot.

But our minds wandered—theirs to marriage and baby-having, mine to an 1840-vintage abandoned log school house less than thirty miles north of Atlanta. It was in easy commuting distance from the office and its three rooms, big living room, a "shedroom" kitchen, and a "loftroom" bedroom, certainly seemed adequate for a woman whose children were grown and gone. I sold the house in town and bought it.

Little did I know that I had experienced only the beginning of child-rearing. My three hadn't gone too far to return—and *bring*. Two husbands, one wife, many babies! I grew so weary of stumbling over bodies on the floor at night I began casting around for another cabin to join to the original one. A neighbor, Ralph Dangar, found it for me, a log cabin of the same size and age three miles down the road from our Sweet Apple settlement in an area near New Home church. We decided to number the logs, tear it down, and move it ourselves with the aid of our faithful carpenter friend, Quinton Johnson. I'll never forget the summer we finally got all the logs moved and stacked in the yard down the hill from Sweet Apple cabin. We had a rainy season to end all rainy seasons. When we went out to look at our logs we found the torrential rains had washed away the numbers!

Nevertheless, with Quinton in charge we got what we subsequently called The Annex up, providing two more bedrooms and a bath. One of the bedrooms is truly a big, open loftroom with space for many grandchildren to sleep dormitory-fashion and even a baby bed for the current youngest.

A family friend, hearing the activity, asked one of my young'uns, "What on earth is your mother doing now? It sounds like she's building Fort Apache!"

And at times it feels like Fort Apache under attack. But I am always glad when the house fills up with family and friends and I believe the two little cabins, built at a time when it was lonely, remote country, are glad, too.

They must have been sad when they stood empty and untenanted for many years, inhabited only by snakes and field mice. They are vocal in the night, old houses are, and the sounds they make are good ones.

We always shift beds around at Sweet Apple when anybody comes. I know people who regard their own beds as sacrosant and, no matter who the guest is, retain the usual for themselves. We always said, "Best for the guest," when I was a child, and the family moved out on the sleeping porch or put down pallets if necessary. So I take it for granted when Sweet Apple cabins begin to fill up that there will be bed changes.

When everybody is sorted out and settled I climb into the old rope bed up under the eaves in the children's room and lie still listening to the tree branches brush the roof, the rush of a mouse between the logs, the whisperings and creakings of people settling in.

A water pipe makes a clanking sound somewhere. I hear the soft bump of the refrigerator door. A whiff of wood smoke from the chimney lingers outside my window. A squirrel, sated by a day-long orgy in the old cherry trees, scrabbles around on the roof.

There is a television set on in one of the bedrooms and a burst of music quickly muted. The phone rings and I hear my daughter answer it and then the pleasant sound of her laughter.

Presently everybody is quiet and I know that most of them are drifting off to sleep. I remember the night light at the foot of the stairs and get up to plug it in. Even I, waking up in my unaccustomed room, could be disoriented in the night and one of them might head for the stairs in the darkness and plunge down them. I find the night light and plug it in and stand a moment looking out the window.

John, the eldest of our teenagers, is still out and the back-porch light, left on to guide him in, makes a pool of silver on grass and tree trunk.

Back in bed the old quilt at the foot looks good to me and I pull it up and begin to get warm and drowsy. Suddenly I am jerked awake by remembering that I took all the really warm blankets off all the other beds, leaving only summer-weight cover and spreads. They might get cold in the night!

Once more, I am out of bed fooling around in the now quiet and dark house, easing extra cover on beds. Susy stirs and a stuffed animal falls off her bed with a gentle "plop." A snore starts across the room and is cut off by the sleeper's turning. There's a car on the road and I wait to see if it will pass by or if its lights will rake the whitewashed log wall, telling me it is in our driveway. It goes on by.

Later, turning on the old rope bed, I hear a car door slam in the backyard. The last wanderer is home. I'll hear the refrigerator door open and close and then his footsteps in the hall and I'll pull the quilt closer and feel happy that the nest is filled once more.

Children can grow up without grandmothers and old cousins. And mothers can manage to provide a living and a home without them. I know this because I see it happening all around me. But I honestly don't see how we would have survived without my mother and her older cousin, a gentle humorous woman we called Sister. They had grown up together, as close as sisters, and by the time my children came along my mother had moved back to the little town of their girlhood and settled in a house she owned across the street from Sister.

So they often arrived together to stay with the children when I had to be away, to lend a hand with nursing when somebody was ill, or just to provide a little excitement in our lives. They themselves had been women-raised children, growing up in a houseful of aunts who were full of vitality and sometimes venom, up to practical jokes and capers until the days of their funerals, when the Irish branches of the family alternated between grief and celebration.

From time to time each of them probably aspired to be what my mother called "saintly, silver-haired" mothers, conducting themselves with vast dignity and decorum. Sister could manage it better than Muv because her reddish hair grayed early. Muv's stayed mostly crow-wing-dark. Sister lacked Muv's venturesomeness, her willingness to catch a bus for anywhere, her yearning to make over and live in every old house she ever saw, her wild mimicry and pleasure in making fun of anybody at any time.

But Sister had her daring moments. Her younger sister, Aunt Toy, had gone to south Florida during the land boom of the 1920s, opened a real estate office, and made what her family believed to be a great deal of money. They never knew for sure because she married a man from Pennsylvania and went up there to live, and the next thing they heard was that she was dead. The widower, a dignified gentleman of advancing years, drove all the way down to Florida to meet his late wife's family and to console and be consoled in her death. That lasted for about a week, and then he asked Sister to marry him.

"She's going to! She's doing it!" I remember hearing Muv tell my father. "I bet he's a regular old Bluebeard, and I know he's a Yankee! Sister must be crazy."

On the contrary, Sister seemed quite happy to risk tying up with Bluebeard and to be the second member of the family since the American Revolution to marry a Yankee.

The marriage didn't last long. I wasn't paying much attention at the time, and I never knew for sure what caused Sister to send the Yankee back to Pennsylvania, a place he referred to as "up to hum." I think it may have been that he was a Bernarr McFadden physical culture nut, a health freak ahead of his time, because he jogged when everybody else was tickled to death to sag somewhere in the shade and take their ease. And he made Sister take brisk hikes through the woods and across the fields despite the fact that she had fallen arches and much walking was very painful to her. On the other hand, it could have been that he deplored the local staples in food-stuff, particularly turnip and collard greens, and ordered "up to hum" for strange cheeses. (He was extremely fond of a limburger which Sister regarded as particularly offensive.)

Anyway, the marriage ended, Sister took back her old name and reinstated her Spanish-American war pension from her first husband, and she and Muv were free to travel to Atlanta to help me rear my children.

They loved shopping in the big stores, riding escalators and elevators and examining their fellow passengers' clothes and general demeanor. They gave names they knew from the Sunday supplements to anybody they considered pretty grand.

"Look, Sister," Muv would whisper. "Yonder goes the Duchess of Windsor!"

"That's Mrs. Astor with her," Sister would say, and they would link arms and prance after their quarries, gig-gling and imitating them.

The children adored these shenanigans, and when the two hatted, white-gloved old ladies stopped at a neighbor-hood spot called Duffy's Tavern for restorative beers on the way home they were totally convulsed.

"Mother, it's a Tech hang-out," they reported to me. "There's not a soul in there over twenty-one, and when Muv and Sister go in there the regulars scatter. I bet they think their mamas have sent for them."

I couldn't help it. I couldn't even help being the butt of their jokes at home. They played different parts every day and cast me in different roles.

One day I would be the Ungrateful Child.

"This is the way it is when you're old," Muv would quaver piteously when the coffee cream ran out and she had to use blue john in her coffee. "Nobody cares about your needs."

Sister would quaver her agreement and they'd both regard me watchfully over their coffee cups, prepared to throw me out of the family if I took them seriously or failed to give my best to the part in which I was cast. So I acted churlish and mean and ordered them to get out of bed and get the scrubbing done.

When that part was played to their satisfaction, they did an about-face and became haughty, high-paying guests.

"I want to complain to the management," Muv informed me grandly. "We're thinking about moving to another hotel unless we can keep the help out of our bed."

All three children and Abel were deployed companionably across their feet.

Or as the morning procession to the bathroom moved raggedly through their room, she would say icily, "Is this what I have to put up with? I understood I was engaging a private bath!"

Their suitcases and assorted boxes and bags from their shopping expeditions filled one end of their room, and they made a commotion over what they called "our goods."

"I hear the management is about to set our goods out on the street," Sister reported to Muv. And then they both rushed to bring me coffee in bed and give me a blouse they had bought me.

They were by turns ingratiating and belligerent. One

minute, Sister would move a little rocker in front of the stack of their possessions and pose as a pitiful old lady who had been evicted from a slum, and the next she had taken over in the kitchen and was turning out a batch of apple tarts.

They would tell me they meant to train Abel as a Seeing Eye dog and take him with them to south Florida where they would get them rich husbands off St. Petersburg's famed green benches. And the next minute they were examining the calendar and assuring me that they couldn't possibly go home. Holidays—Arbor Day or Groundhog Day or something like that—were coming up, and they couldn't think of leaving us on so festive an occasion.

And when they left we missed them acutely. Three generations under one roof, said Mary, counting up, made life much livelier.

Muv had strange ways of making a point with children, and one of her most fearsome instruments was name-calling. Sometimes it wasn't quite clear to me why your soul shrivels when she called you by the name of some long-dead cousin or aunt—a shoddy character, of course. It happened when I was a child, and of course she turned the same technique on my children. I suppose it was the combination of contempt and sorrow that she put in her tone.

She could do the same thing in the pathos department. A few years ago she felt sorry for me and was outraged at some trivial demand the children made of me. One of those last-straw things, probably, like the time a cousin of ours who had borne up bravely through all kinds of vicissitudes went to pieces when her child reversed his course on the way to school and came back home with his shoe sole flapping.

"No! No! No!" she screeched and had to be given sedatives and put to bed.

I don't remember what the straw laid on my back was, but I remember Muv's saying to the children, "That's right! Let the old work ox do it! She's nothing but a work ox, let her do it!"

"A what?" they asked, puzzled. And half the lesson was lost while Muv took off from her anger to explain to them, children of the tractor age, about oxen.

I was indignant that she was making them feel guilty. I didn't like the metaphor much, either. When I feel martyred and put-upon, which is right regularly, I like to think of myself as a fragile, dark-pain-filled-eyes type, bearing and doing beyond my strength. Not a muscular, heavy-haunched ox.

I needn't have worried. My children felt no guilt, and they promptly shortened the appellation "work ox" to "old W.O."

Not long after that, Mary, the open-everything-early child in our family, the one who can't bear to wait for birthdays and Christmases without sneaking at least a premature peek, came to my room at bedtime in her pajamas, her hair rolled up in those little snails girls used to endure for curls.

"Mother," she asked, "do you really mind getting surprises early?"

I stalled for time, trying to figure out the occasion. Not birthday, not Christmas; what comes in late January? Finally I capitulated, and she brought forth one of those beautiful dime-store hearts, hollow chocolate embossed with L-O-V-E.

"It's beautiful," I exclaimed, reaching for it. But she held it out at a little distance, the better to let me see the full inscription: "Love to W.O."

She grinned mischievously and I lifted a hand to hit her, but I didn't. I may be the only mother in America who gets called a lumbering dumb beast of burden on a valentine. But as long as it is said tenderly and in chocolate, why should I complain?

To this day when I am doing something for one of the grandchildren that seems a bit above and beyond, one of my children will say cheerfully, "Look at old W.O. go!"

We lost two babies in infancy. Mary's first, a little boy named Richard, was a fine, laughing, apparently healthy baby of three months when I went by their apartment one night at seven o'clock. He was dead at midnight from that horror called SIDS: Sudden Infant Death Syndrome, or "crib death."

Jimmy's little boy, Jamie, was in the care of a trusted nursemaid, the daughter of his in-laws' longtime friend and servant. One afternoon when both parents were away at their respective jobs she called in a panic. Their Jamie had fallen out of his crib and struck his head on the rocker of a little red chair I had given him. He was dead within an hour after they got him to the hospital.

The pain we suffered is with us still and will probably last as long as we all live. I don't believe you forget a detail of such anguish or ever stop asking, "How did it happen? Why?"

Robust, vigorous little ones come along, but you can't help looking at them searchingly, fearfully. Are they really all right? Or will they one day fall prey to some hidden malady, some hideous happenstance?

Five other children were born to Mary and Susan, and we were almost lulled into thinking the fearsome child-taker had passed us by. They were beautiful and strong. John, born in February; Charles, called Bird, in July; sweet Sibley, the first girl, born the following June; Ted, the following November; and Susy, the winsome little ca-boose, in August, eight years after her brother John and six years after her brother Ted. They had illnesses and narrow escapes. John almost cut his hand off at a Boy Scout meeting in a church recreation hall. The night run to the hospital emergency room was fairly routine in both families. But they all flourished.

Mary's David, child of a second marriage, was in the same pattern, a sturdy, stalwart fellow we weren't going to have to worry about. But Mary did worry. The old specter had come back to haunt her, and many a night she gave up sleep entirely to sit by his bed and watch him breathe. It was illogical, but we all felt it in a measure. Then his little brother John Steven arrived—prematurely. Our fears were justified. Except for the wisdom of and quick rush to the operating room by a woman doctor who happened to be on duty when Mary was taken to the hospital in the middle of the night, both she and the baby would have died.

He was almost the prettiest of all our young'uns, John Steven, with a clarity of face and features that seems to be special to Cesarian babies. He was not red or wrinkled, no wizened old man, but fair and clear-eyed with the radiance of an angel. They gave him a blood transfusion and kept him in the hospital for a few days after his mother was released, and he seemed fine when he went home.

Then one night his brother David cried out in his sleep, and Mary went to check on him. On her way back to bed she laid a hand on the little baby, although he was quiet and apparently sleeping well. His small face was cold. She turned on the light and he was blue. It was the old nightmare repeating itself.

She started screaming and Ron, pulled out of a deep sleep, stumbled to her side, grabbed the baby from her arms, and began giving him mouth-to-mouth resuscitation. Moments later they had him in the hospital.

It was the old, mysterious, unexplainable murderer back: SIDS.

Thus began a series of hospital stays for John Steven and, of course, for all of us. He had the attention of teams of exceptional physicians, people already engaged in trying to determine and conquer the causes of infant deaths. He was examined and tested and treated with the best the doctors knew about. He was in and out of intensive care and harnessed to a machine called a monitor which would sound an alarm if his breathing stopped. And sometimes it did. Lights would flash, an alarm would sound, and those of us waiting beside him were jolted to our feet and into terror once more.

Susan came from New Jersey to help us through the emergency. Ron's mother, Jean, came from Alexandria.

David spent days and nights with us in the country, and after a time the crisis, although still with us, seemed manageable, even acceptable. John Steven was going to have to live with a monitor, but they believed he was going to live.

One night he seemed much better. The little machine with its winking eye was silent. All his vital signs were satisfactory to his doctors and nurses, and things were generally quiet at Henrietta Egleston Hospital for Children. The nurse in charge, looking at the wan weary faces of the baby's parents, urged them to go home. Get some rest, she told them. Nurses on the hall had few other patients that night. They would stay close to John Steven; they would be vigilant.

Mary and Ron were glad to go home and to be with David, and I thought I was glad to go home to sleep for a change. But at 3 A.M. my sleep was unaccountably broken. I found myself wide awake.

It was a bright moonlight night, and I went to the window and inspected the silvered bushes and rough grass in the yard, the shadow tracery on the rooftops of well house and toolshed.

Thirty miles away a little baby slept or cried or struggled for breath. Our little baby. Alone.

I called the hospital, and the nurse on duty said he was fine. There had been no alarms. He was sleeping soundly.

So I wandered around the house some more, standing in the dark to be able to see the moonswept yard, then turning on the light to try to read. But I kept thinking of him, his small translucent face with the clear eyes, the smooth round head, the curve of the little body and the feel of it when you held it to your shoulder.

It took me five minutes to get dressed and maybe forty to drive the nearly deserted expressway to town. Once I made a wrong turn and was lost for a little while. Once I stopped for gas and found the filling station closed. Lights in the parking garage next to the hospital seemed pallid against the moonlight. There was no attendant on duty at that hour, but a uniformed security guard directed me to a parking space and then walked with me to the hospital building and unlocked a side door to let me in.

The halls were quiet. The nurses' station near John Steven's room was occupied by a handful of young women, examining charts, talking softly. They looked up when they heard my footsteps and they smiled.

"He's all right," one of them said. "He's having a good night. It's almost time for his bottle. If you'd care to give it to him, it would be a help."

She didn't need my help, I knew. She was being nice to a fool of a grandmother who didn't have sense enough to stay home and sleep. I've always abhorred the idea that I would ever want to feel needed. And yet when I lifted John Steven and sat down in the rocker with him I felt content. He snuggled against my shoulder while we waited for his bottle and made snuffling, hungry baby noises. I may have imagined that he knew one of his family—his blood kin, as we say in the south—was with him. But I felt enormously relieved and happy.

While John Steven's health was so precarious, David's bloomed, and I had to learn all over again that putting a baby to bed is one of the most challenging tasks in the world. Women should have known centuries ago that they could do absolutely anything, become editors, engi-

neers, inventors, soldiers, sailors, surgeons, prime ministers, miners, scientists, because they had trained on something tougher—getting young'uns settled for the night.
The trouble is that it's like childbirth or climbing Mount
Everest. When the struggle is over, you forget what it
was like.

The early part of the evening lulls you into thinking
you've got it made. The late-day capers over the grass in
pursuit of a ball or the dogs, suppertime and bath time
and hammock time, are all velvet. You prepare a bottle
(his comfort, his soporific, although he is now eighteen
months old and can drink out of a cup) and you bear him
up to bed, bathed and powdered and drowsy (you hope)
at 8 P.M.

At first all is quiet and, glowing with self-congratula-
tion, you clean up the kitchen and plan a leisurely bath.
Then you hear the bottle hit the floor, followed by the
soft plunk of the teddy bear. The slats of the crib creak
complainingly. The air is rent by howls. The house is either on fire or he is being attacked by bears and alligators.

"Let him cry it out," my daughter had instructed me.
So I hovered at the foot of the stairs, wringing my hands
and listening. The tone changed. He was no longer frightened of demons. He was angry. He hollered and
screeched, and there was accusation in every note. You
know you have done something wrong, and you plod up
the stairs to see.

Yep, his diaper needed changing and it was all my
fault. He wriggled with delight over the operation, kicking
me playfully in the stomach, whooping with pleasure at
the sight of me.

Once more you put baby and bottle and teddy bear in

the bed and return to your listening post on the bottom step of the stairs. All goes well for a while. He sings and rocks the bed. Then he lets out an experimental cry. You are unmoved. He cries again, neither in anger nor in censure but because he is sad and lonely, a neglected waif, an orphan, Oliver Twist crying in the night. You swallow hard and dry your damp hands on your apron. Maybe he's winding down. Maybe in a minute he'll go to sleep. He doesn't. The piteous wails tear at your heart.

Once more, up the stairs.

He was jubilant at the sight of me. He wound his arms around my neck, nestled his head against my shoulder.

"Bocka, bocka," he said softly, and I knew "rocker" when I heard it. I obediently took him to the old Brumby chair on the porch.

Darkness was beginning to settle on the woods. The birds made sleepy sounds. We rocked, we sang, and finally I filled a fresh bottle and stuck on a fresh diaper and hauled him up the stairs again. It was an uneasy quiet for a time—but it was quiet. Waiting, listening, I found my back aching, my clothes drenched with sweat. It seemed hours before I dared to tiptoe up the stairs to check.

He was a rose and gold Botticelli angel, the most beautiful thing in the world—a sleeping baby. It was 9 P.M.

A lot of sappy and not-so-sappy things have been written about a baby's smile. Frank L. Stanton, the Georgia poet, in the song "Mighty Lak' a Rose," advanced the opinion that a baby's smile "makes you feel that heaven's coming straight to you." James M. Barrie contended in *Peter Pan* that when the first baby laughed the first time, "the laugh broke into a thousand pieces and they all went skipping about, and that was the beginning of fairies."

Personally, I felt it easy to resist the urge to carry on about babies' smiles until we noticed that John Steven, although apparently recovering, never smiled. He seemed amiable and good-humored enough, but he simply did not smile. The usual chin-chucking, goochee-goo tricks that grown-ups try on infants left him bored and withdrawn. He still wore a harness around his middle connected to a monitor on the wall so we could keep tabs on his breathing. The fire station down at the corner, the power company, and the Heart Association all knew that he was a SIDS baby and could have trouble. But he seemed to be doing all right. He was rosily gaining weight and lengthening out. He simply didn't smile. He inspected us with a certain wariness, but he didn't think our antics were deliciously funny, and he didn't feel any social compulsion to make us think he did.

It was all right with me. Some people, like former President Jimmy Carter, use a smile as a trademark. Some, if you'll forgive me, use it as the song directs, for an umbrella. Some people believe if you smile the world smiles with you and stuff like that. John Steven hadn't been around long enough to be subjected to anybody's sunshiny philosophical clichés. He didn't smile, and I didn't fault him for it.

Then the doctors started asking if he smiled. Since his hospital stay he had been seeing doctors with the frequency of a Park Avenue hypochondriac. Every day or so he saw some doctor about some aspect of his problems. And every time one or the other of them would ask, "Does he smile?"

His mother said he did but she said it uncertainly, and I

suspected that she was seeing a smile in any of his grimaces. Sometimes wet pants bring an expression to a baby's face that a mother can interpret as a smile. Sometimes gas on his stomach does it. So I wasn't sure and began to worry. Some of the viruses babies get before or immediately after birth have long-range and sad results— blindness, deafness, mental retardation, to name a few. If he didn't smile, did that mean he was subject to one of these?

The whole family began to worry. His aunt and cousins called from New Jersey to ask, "Is John smiling yet?" His other grandparents called from Virginia. I went by and played with him and covertly, not wanting to make a big deal out of it, made faces and told jokes and jiggled him. He regarded me with grave disapproval.

What happened I do not know, but one morning he decided to smile. A dimple appeared in his cheek, his lips curved back to show his toothless gums, his eyes sparkled with merriment, and he said, "Oooooh!"

Having got the hang of it, he did it again and again. The sight of his parents' faces put him in stitches. The arrival of his breakfast caused him to light up like a Christmas tree. When he lay in his crib and looked at the ceiling he smiled to himself over a new idea or some old remembered joke. Who knows?

The doctors didn't say so, but we couldn't help regarding that smile as a lovely omen. That's why, perhaps, so many corny things have been written about a baby's smile in the past.

E ven as Susy commanded that I be an instructive grandmother, I had to acknowledge that I owe the children in the family some return on all they've taught me. Ted taught me to eat ketchup on French fries, for instance, a culinary discovery which has been a great boon to me.

Ted's Uncle Jimmy was the first one to remind me that some of adversity's sweet uses are minor ones, like not despairing when you can't sleep at night. Once, when he was a little boy, some friends in California awakened the household with an early-morning call at that precious pre-dawn hour when sleep seems its deepest and best. They just wanted to say "hello," and they said it until we were all fully awake.

When the conversation ended, I sat by the phone feeling yawny and depleted and undecided what to do with the fragile ragtag left of the night.

"We could eat some cereal," my son offered. "You want a bowl of cereal or a cup of coffee?"

"No milk," I pointed out. "You drank it for supper."

"We could get some," he suggested. "The fruit stand's open all night."

The paper was on the porch. The dog had awakened at his post by the front door and was yawning and shaking himself. A bird tuned up in the sweet-gum tree in the back yard. The night was softly and subtly turning to day.

"There ought to be a sunrise," Jimmy said. "Would you like to see it?"

I looked at the bed longingly. After all, I've seen sunrises. And then I looked at his face. His sisters had tumbled back into bed without really coming alive, but he was wide awake and like the dog, Abel, young enough and curious enough to want to be abroad in the world, sniffing the air and admiring the shapes and colors of the town in this foreign early-morning light.

"Let me get into some clothes," I said.

It's such a pleasant thing to watch the city bestir itself. We waved at the street cleaner, who, with barrel cart and broom, tidied the gutters of Peachtree Street. We saw paper boys finishing their rounds and truckers starting out. We drove to the top of a hill and saw the sun slip up in a blaze of color through the trees over in the park.

And then we went home and had coffee and marveled that a phone call in the night could so change the dimensions of a day.

It wasn't necessary for the children to teach me to value children. As an only child myself, I grew up envious of big families and with a high regard for all young'uns. Not so my daughter Susan. She had to learn to like children from her own.

Susan was a kind and competent baby-sitter whose services were always in demand among our friends, although they recognized that unlike her sister she baby-sat for money, not out of an o'er-weening affection for little ones. Even when she went to the hospital to have John, she stoutly maintained that it would be cheaper, easier, and more fun if they got a cocker spaniel instead. John changed her.

She took up children, loving and admiring them and enjoying not only her own baby but the babies of others, marveling at their swift development, their various abilities and charms. In fact, she may have been in danger of swapping her youthful detachment for real mushy-headiness if it hadn't been for Ted.

Ted, who became the most amiable and companionable of teenagers, was born on Election Day, an act I considered sheer perversity. Why couldn't he have let his mother vote before he decided to come? For a few years he was a model of perversity, the reddest of our redheads, the angriest of Angry Young Men. He scorned baby talk. In fact, he scorned communication of any kind until he was over a year old. Then his first words came in a clear, well-rounded imperative. His mother was playing the piano and she sprang a song on him.

"Don't sing!" Ted ordered.

The only time I, his loving grandmother, was ever allowed to hold Ted was when he was debilitated by illness, suffering a raging fever, and due at the doctor's office momentarily. The rest of the time he brushed off babyish cuddling and devoted himself to such enterprises as putting sand in the piano or dropping the family silver down the sewer.

With a child like that I fully expected Susan to revert to her old attitude that babies are more trouble and less pleasure than puppies. But she doted on Ted. She really liked him, and occasionally I'd catch her viewing him with a mixture of awe and incredulity.

One day she reported to me that he had been watching bumblebees on television. She was pleased to see the depth of his concentration and hopeful that it was the beginning of a happy association between Ted and the great baby-sitter. Then she heard him say, loud and clear, "Hit him back, stupid!"

We were all staggered. Where, oh, where, did a two-year-old get such talk? Was television to blame, his older brother, or some bad companion like an aggressive three-year-old?

Secretly, I felt a little set up to behold that new and vigorous blood in the family. As a longtime pacifist and exponent of turn-the-other-cheek, it cheered me that we had a fighter. Nobody admires spirit as much as the mealymouthed. I didn't want Ted to know it, but I said hooray for "Hit him back, stupid!"

Three years later Ted became an author, pasting up, writing, and illustrating a volume with the title "Hate at All Times."

John introduced me to football. I met it briefly when I was in school, of course, but when I stopped knowing the members of the team I stopped paying any attention to the game. John loved it from the time he was eight years old, and I began to go with his mother to watch him play when he was twelve or thirteen. I found all that tumbling around on the ground, the heaps of flailing bodies, confusing and a little frightening.

"Don't play that dumb game, honey," I begged him out of my vast prejudice. "They'll knock out your teeth and break your bones. Pay attention to English and History and forget football."

"Let him alone, Mother," my daughter Susan advised. "As long as he's interested in football he's not drinking beer or smoking pot. He's jogging and lifting weights to take care of that old body."

Beer drinking and pot smoking were real problems in some of our schools then, even some of our elementary schools. It was disturbing and heartbreaking and I wanted no part of it for our children, so I subsided. It was true that his physical well-being was important to John—as a means of getting on that rough turf on Friday afternoon and knocking down what appeared to me to be nice young fellows who had done nothing to antagonize him except that they wore muddy, grass-stained uniforms of a different color from his and showed an inordinate interest in gaining possession of a very commonplace-looking little ball.

Still, I went to games in preference to other forms of social activity. Friends asked me to parties, sometimes to meet celebrities like Erma Bombeck and a Saudi prince and princess.

"I'm so sorry," I would regret automatically. "We're playing Westminster Friday night."

That "we" shows you. I wasn't playing anybody. I was sitting on a hard bleachers seat, sometimes in an electrical storm, sometimes in sleet or record-breaking heat, worrying myself to death over things I didn't understand, like "first downs" and "conversions," which had nothing to do with either failure as I knew it or religious experience or exchanging your foreign money.

John's parents and brother and sister moved away to New Jersey when he was a high school junior, but he stayed behind in boarding school, not because he couldn't bear to be separated from his beloved school and dear relations but because he held varsity status here. If he went to New Jersey he couldn't play varsity football for a whole year!

"For goodness' sake," I said when I heard. "That's nothing to determine where you're going to live and go to school. A game!"

John didn't deign to argue against such ignorance and insensitivity, and I was, of course, glad that he stayed behind because he spent weekends with me, moving in when football season was over. The presence of that big boy in the house at night was comforting and cheering. His humor brightened my days, the logs he cut and hauled for the fireplace brightened my nights. As a result, I went to a lot of his football games by myself when I couldn't round up family or friends to go.

A man friend was with me the night John was injured while playing. An old football player in his youth, he kept up with the game far better than I did, and before I saw it, he said quietly, "John's been hurt."

John's lessons to me kept me in my seat. I had long since learned that female relatives were not wanted many places but especially on the football field or hanging over the fence behind the players' bench. With remarkable self-control I did not go plunging down on the field but sat very still watching coaches and a doctor moving with deliberate speed toward a great muddy hulk of a boy who lay on the ground, looking, from where I sat, awfully quiet and very vulnerable.

They leaned over him while the clock on the scoreboard stopped, and then two of his teammates hauled him to the bench and stretched him out there, using his helmet to elevate his right foot and a spare football as a pillow for his head. I was so caught up in the devices they were using for succoring a fallen comrade that I didn't worry for about a minute.

"I hope John hasn't broken his foot," Jack said.

Suddenly the antiquated business of no-place-for-a-woman outraged me.

"Go see," I said desperately. "Go down there and ask the doctor. You can go; you're a man."

It was gall for me to say it, but I had to know.

The report was slow coming back. My friend spoke to the coach and the doctor and leaned over and said something to John. He signaled to me, an airy wave of the hand I knew was meant to reassure, to say John was all right. But looking at my big young'un stretched out in that ludicrous arrangement of helmet and football, I didn't see how he could possibly be all right. He was out of the game, wasn't he?

Jack didn't come back to his seat, and I had to know more. I packed up that gear you take to games—cushion, raincoat, thermos jug—and worked my way down to the fence.

"Is John hurt bad?" I asked Jack.

It wasn't easy getting his attention. He mumbled something about an intercepted pass and I realized he was doing the unthinkable, paying no attention to John but *watching the game!* I looked at John, and he had lifted his head from the football pillow and was doing the same.

The next morning the doctor looked at X-rays and told us John's injury was a sprain. (Turned out later it was a cracked bone, but we didn't know that until he had played five or six more games.) I hauled gallons of scalding water to him all weekend and he was docile about soaking the injured ankle for, guess what reason, he had to get back to practice!

The male animal, I decided, is totally incomprehensible to me, and they were welcome to their old "place."

The season by rights should have been over when my editor, Mr. Lawrence P. Ashmead, came to Atlanta just before Christmas. But it wasn't, because the team perversely wouldn't stop winning. It won and won and went into something called playoffs and won again and again, and the night Mr. Ashmead was due in town there was a final major effort by John's Woodward Academy to wrest the championship from Marist, a school which had beat them early in the season.

The writing community of Atlanta was horrified that we had a New York editor on the hoof in our midst and I proposed to haul him off to a high school football game. Every single one of my literary friends could think of better uses of an editor's time, mostly, I suspected, discussing markets, contracts, and the publishability of their manuscripts. But my young'un was playing football and I had to be there, and all I could do was explain and invite.

"It's the state championship," I said tentatively, "and John—"

"Oh, I know," Mr. Ashmead said warmly. "We have to see that."

"You'll go with us?" I said humbly. John's Aunt Mary and Uncle Ron were going too.

"I'd like that very much," he said. "I don't know anything about football, but I certainly wouldn't want to miss John's game."

The friends who felt that a literary gentleman might feel more comfortable in a cozy bar or even discussing best-sellers over hot tea were certainly right where physical comfort was concerned. Marist School's athletic field was windy and cold, its bleachers jammed, especially on the side allotted to the visiting team's fans, which is what we were. The elbows of the people beside us were in our ribs, the knees of those behind us were in our backs, and every time we leaped to our feet we knocked the earmuffs of the gentleman in front.

Because he said he was unacquainted with football, I felt compelled to share my meager knowledge with my friend.

"Those things over yonder are goal posts," I said. "That lighted sign is the scoreboard. That oval thing they're jostling over so rudely is the football. Those boys are the Woodwards, those the Marists, and in that jersey with seventy-four on his back . . ."

He said he had already spotted our boy John, and he settled down to listen and to look with an expression of gentle interest and courteous attention on his face.

Well, the game didn't go well for our team for almost all the first half. Mary and Ron were so nervous they kept going off and bringing back hot coffee. They couldn't bear to watch the activities on the field. I wished my Number One grandson was a crossword puzzle or table tennis addict instead of a big tackle.

Then the tide turned.

The Marist eleven was breathing on Woodward's goal posts. What is known as Woodward's "dee-fense" went in to keep them from scoring.

Suddenly I felt wild movement at my side and heard a

voice bellowing, "Hold that line, Big Red!"

The editor from New York was on his feet going crazy.

"Stop 'em, Big Red!" the normally soft-spoken Mr. Ashmead thundered again.

Well, it was soon history. Big Red, as they call the Woodward team, did stop 'em, and there was much rejoicing by all hands on our side of the field and in our family. And I am still marveling at the adaptability of New Yorkers. How can I persuade John that you don't pronounce "defense" "*dee*-fense" when he has the example of an editor to bolster him in that usage?

"Christmas won't be Christmas without any presents," observed Jo March in the classic opening line of *Little Women*. I have had a hard time convincing myself that it wouldn't be Christmas without children. Of course it would. That most holy and reverent of days comes to old and young alike, sometimes with more meaning to the old.

By now we have had many Christmases in our family, and I have loved them all. The wartime Christmas when Jimmy and Susan were babies, toys were in short supply, and the teddy bear came wearing a soldier suit. The first Christmas after the war, when we had followed the children's father to a newspaper job in Florida and lived in a fishing camp. Our turkey had to be cooked by a baker in town because we had only a little tin oven which fit over one of our gas plate's two burners, and it kept going only so long as you fed quarters to a meter. We had no lights or ornaments for our funny little tree, so we decorated with Christmas cards from friends back in Georgia—maybe the most meaningful ornaments we ever had because each card was like the hand of a friend reaching out and touching us. We pooled dinner with the other residents of the fishing camp and afterwards wandered through a hedge of madly blooming hibiscus to fill a washtub with oranges and grapefruit from a friend's orchard.

It's a well-known fact that you seldom remember the gifts you give or get at Christmas. There have been a few major and memorable ones, of course. The Cloud Nine coat for Susan when she was fourteen was one.

We went shopping for a plain serviceable navy blue coat in the fall, and Susan saw what was new that year, a fleecy coat of silver gray nylon, soft as a kitten's ear and stunning on her with her red hair and gray eyes. It was priced at $99.95. We had $25 to spend.

We both knew that it was out of the question, but Susan tried it on anyhow and she had an idea.

"Mother, could we put it on the layaway and let me baby-sit it out?"

Baby-sitters made 25 or at most 50 cents an hour in those days, and I knew the coat would be outgrown or out of style before Susan ever raised that much money. But from the way her eyes rested on it, the way her fingers caressed it, I knew she had to try.

We paid the $25 down and Susan, wearing her shabby, too-small last year's coat, took every baby-sitting assignment that turned up. By Christmas she had paid $30 more on the coat. It was the halfway mark only, and the family budget wasn't going to be equal to redeeming it. After all, there were the other two to buy presents for.

But Jimmy and Mary had already decided that we had to get the coat for Susan, no matter what, and each of them came to me separately to discuss it and to offer to stint on their own Santa Claus. I don't remember what they got and I doubt if they do, but we did make a secret trip to town and paid out the coat. When Susan opened it on Christmas morning, the sight of her face was Christmas enough for all of us.

It was our custom to go to the church's carol service on Christmas morning, and of course Susan wore the coat. To her chagrin—and ours—the old stone church was not rocked by her new splendor. The organ played, the choir sang, the minister read the Christmas story, and friends smiled and said, "Merry Christmas." But nobody seemed to be aware of the coat. As we were leaving, we paused in the vestibule to speak to Dr. Vernon Broyles, the minister, and he took Susan's hand in one of his and patted her sleeve with the other.

"Beautiful, Susan," he murmured. "Beautiful."

It justified the waiting and the baby-sitting and the last-minute, all-out family push.

We all beamed at Dr. Broyles, and Susan wore the coat until she went off to college. Then I think she slept under it.

Some years you think you're not going to make it through Christmas. I had that feeling when the children were small. We had no car, and I had to bring three little red rocking chairs home on the bus. The bus was crowded, and the other passengers might have been appalled to see a woman get on with red rockers bristling over her shoulder and sticking out over her elbows. But they smiled and made room and helped me and the little chairs fit into the bus somehow.

The years after the children were married and away were going to be the worst, I always thought. But the most fun we ever had in preparation may have been the filling of a trunk for Mary and her family when they lived in California. I had acquired the old trunk at an auction. Susan and I painted it and had its lock repaired, and then we spent weeks contriving special wrappings for each small gift that went into it. The gifts themselves have been forgotten—except for the oilcloth landing field and the airport we made for Bird, who was at the age of three wildly enamoured of "aa-planes." (The next year we progressed to astronaut suits, bought at F.A.O. Schwarz's on a gala and unexpected trip to New York to be on the *Today* show.) But most of all I savor the memory of the evenings we sat at Susan's dining-room table with paper and paints and glue, making packages that looked like bears and puppies and baby dolls.

Sometimes it seems to me that I am slower to learn how to get ready for Christmas than any woman should be. By now I am a veteran Christmas celebrant and I should be competent, if not always inspired. But there never seems to be time or leisure for organization. Instead, I shuffle about in a maelstrom of started-and-unfinished tasks, snippets of paper and ribbon, knitting wool and scraps of sewing. The housecleaning is never done by the time friends are holding their wassail parties and open houses. The baking and shopping are behind, the tree trimming and wreath hanging last-minute.

Not long ago I tottered home from town on a December evening with splitting shopping bags, armloads of sharp-cornered boxes, and aching feet and fell into bed, only to awaken in the middle of the night overwhelmed by the things I had done, the things I had not done. Oh, it's going to be a terrible Christmas, I thought mournfully, turning restlessly under the too-hot electric blanket. I didn't get anything good for Susan. Sibley, my eldest granddaughter, was going to hate her handbag; it was small, and aren't teenagers into big bags this year? Or vice versa? The big synonym book I thought was such a great present for Bird would probably split its wrappings and be lost in the mail.

It's the worst collection of presents anybody ever got from me, I decided. That was bad enough, but I hit the roster of people I still hadn't shopped for, which was worse. The clock said 2 A.M., and I couldn't go back to sleep.

There was nothing to do but to turn on the lights and put on coffee and resume the fight to get things ready. The big needlepoint Christmas stocking I made for Susy in the spring should by that time be hanging by their fireplace in New Jersey, but I didn't even have it lined. The red velvet I bought was definitely the wrong shade for lining, killing the red of the needlepoint. I should have got green.

The heat whispered from the furnace. A light rain was

falling on the roof. I waited for the coffee and picked up a little stack of Christmas cards I'd been too tired to open the night before.

"Be of love a little more mindful," one of them said.

Maybe it was an early-morning rush of energy. But the tiredness and the woebegoneness dropped away. Presents bought or made, presents mailed or not mailed, delivered or not delivered—are they really all that important? Somehow we always get through the urgent pre-Christmas days, and next year we won't remember what we got or gave this year.

But there are gifts to remember, especially in that year which was rapidly drawing to a close. There was the rich and sustaining friendship of many people, their kindness and help: miracles, really. I listened to the rain and thought about the littlest baby in our family, who lived because of the skill and caring of doctors and nurses at four Atlanta hospitals. I thought of Mary's neighbors who teamed up, organized, and brought her and Ron and the babies dinner every day for ten days, when she came home from the hospital. I thought of the firemen at the corner who said, "Yes, we know your house. If your baby stops breathing we can be there in less than two minutes." I thought of the couples next door to Mary and down the street who volunteered to take the cardiac-pulmonary resuscitation course from the Red Cross so they could revive John Steven if necessary.

Later the sun came up and turned the frost on the old corncrib to quicksilver. I sang as I scrawled the address on a misshapen package. The thing you have to do about Christmas—the only thing, really—is to remember that it is the season for love and gratitude first of all and that the immensity of those things transcends wearying little concerns.

We never really believed that Susan and Edward and the children would go to faraway New Jersey to live. Edward's job took him there and for a time he commuted, always with the knowledge in the back of his head that they would sooner or later move there. We didn't believe it because we didn't want to.

We were dependent on them. They lived in an old house close to town in what was Atlanta's first suburban development, handy for drop-in visits, although Mary and I didn't make them as often as we now wish we had.

There was occasionally a little space of time when husbands had gone to work, children were still asleep, and the three of us sat around the little table in Susan's kitchen, drinking coffee and talking—what they used to call "grown-up lady time." Susy, wearing ruffled underpants and nothing else, might wander in, followed by the dogs, Sarah, George, and Samantha. The sun laid tentative early-morning fingers of light along the black branches of the big oak tree outside the window. The coffee was hot and fresh, the little pottery bowl of flowers on the table a colorful reminder of the small garden Susan and her neighbor cultivated on a vacant lot.

We talked of trips and children, of schools and books, laughing together, often at one another but with gentle tolerance. Work-bound traffic picked up on a street a block away and, listening, I knew it was time to leave them. I collected my things and stood a minute at the door, reluctant to go, reluctant to have this space of time together vanish.

Time passes, people change, the little piece of morning and talk and laughter will be no more. There will be other times, of course, but not this time. The trouble in families nowadays, I thought, is that there isn't enough time for meeting. You are birds of passage, always on the fly, meeting briefly if at all, checking in and out with one another as if you were dealing with one of those toll-free reservation numbers. If there is trouble, you make time for one another. If there is occasion for celebration, you will work it out somehow. But the moments to sit and talk of nothing much, to laugh together and watch the light on walls, to savor one another's presence . . . these are rare moments, so rare it behooves us to recognize them and to cherish them.

The children came to the country to stay while their parents went to New Jersey to house-hunt, and it was pleasure for them and for me. There were times when I wondered how the mother of three children managed without full-time help. Looking back to their mother's childhood, I was indebted to Bessie Galloway, who was there when I was at work, coping with laundry and meals and screeches of "Make her stop!" and "He made that noise again!" Their mother copes with no Bessie—and so did I this time.

Sometimes I wondered a little wistfully what happened to the custom of children slipping off to the swimming hole by themselves—this when I had to gather up suits and towels and head for the car. Sometimes I wondered why I never got around to reading *Diddie, Dumps and Tot* and *The Secret Garden* to Susy or getting Ted to teach me to play chess. The sumptuous meals I meant to cook to ignite John's praise seemed to never turn out that way.

But we muddled through, and Susy and I got in some prime walks. The woods were deep and dark as we came home late one afternoon, and Susy paused and tugged at my hand.

"Listen!" she whispered. "I hear a snake!"

I listened, and the sound she heard was crickets and July flies sawing away in the trees.

"That's not a snake, Susy," I said. "That's the sound of summertime."

"What's the sound of summertime?" she asked.

It's many things, I told her, and tried to enumerate them. It's the sound of cicadas in the trees and the soft murmurous voice of a warm breeze in the pines. It's the hanging baskets dripping water under the eaves after their late afternoon watering, the ice-cream freezer turning, the creaky windy song the electric fan sings on the back porch. It's the sound of the lawnmower, the sudden rush of a martin's passage as he nabs a low-flying bug on the wing.

It's the snick of the hoe in the garden, the crack of a ripe watermelon beneath a knife blade, the tinkle of ice in tea glasses. It's the skittering rush of a blue-tailed skink across a rock wall, the whine of a mosquito in a quiet room. It's the plop of a frog in a quiet lake as noisy, bathing-suited children arrive for a swim, the sweet cool chantey of water pouring over a dam.

Summertime is children's voices singing all the old-fashioned hymns at vacation Bible school and all the funny ditties at day camp. It's the plunk of ripe plums and blackberries in a picker's basket, the creak of a swing chain. It's the sound of a boy's bare foot reaching for and finding a barky resting place high in an oak tree.

Summertime has a special cadence when you can almost hear the corn grow and the earth turn on its axis. A ripening apple lets go and hits the ground with a soft thud, a lightning bug lifts a lantern in the dogwood tree, and you feel that you must have heard the flick of a tiny switch.

Not all summertime sounds are gentle and rhythmic. There's the high squeal of the little girl who missed a thrown ball, the authoritative smack of the boy's mitt which caught it.

Maybe the summertime noise I will remember best in years to come is of Susy, then "five and eleven-twelfth years old," as she put it, rushing over the yard in pursuit of a scrawny flea-bitten hound somebody dropped off on our road. She thought he was beautiful and gave him a lovely name.

"Rainbow! Rainbow!" She sang the word like a litany in the still sunny air.

It was never my desire to have my children grow old and shriveled in my service, as my friend Maggie used to put it. I wanted no long-suffering old maids around to hand me my liniment and wince over my carping and whining. I wanted no old bachelor son to valiantly tell people "Mom is my best girl," while hating my guts.

When it came time for my children to flee the nest I

had a pang or two but I resolutely gave them the requisite push, knowing my duty when I saw it. And I have never stopped missing them.

It suits me very well for them to be off in homes of their own, I keep saying, but it suits me even better to have them arrive for a visit.

Susan was coming down from New Jersey and it was like all the homecomings they have made through the years. When they went to camp or to their grandmother's house or to boarding school I always reached a high pitch of excitement over their return.

Not long ago I had just finished seeing off a batch of house guests and was feeling pretty tired but I told Mary, the Atlanta one, that I had to hurry home to get ready for Susan.

"Aw, Mama, you don't," she said. "You can relax about Susan. She doesn't care if the house is clean or not and you all can go out for a hamburger. Go home and take a nap."

It was a sound suggestion and I considered it. Briefly. But it would have been impossible to do it. Mothers have to Get Ready for returning children, no matter their age. I remember nearly falling out of a very high kitchen window, trying to get it clean for Jimmy's return when he was a 16-year-old boy coming home from military school. Would he care if the windows were clean? Of course not. But I had to do it. I sat on the sill with my feet in the sink, leaning out over a 20-foot drop, and scrubbed and scrubbed and sang my favorite Thanksgiving hymn, "Come Ye Thankful People Come."

This time I mopped the kitchen and washed my good rag rugs and cut some white sasanquas for the little vase on the bedside table. The afternoon was warm, but home-coming in November calls for a fire on the hearth so I hauled out ashes and hauled in firewood.

Supper was simple and quick, and we all went to bed early, but I awakened before dawn with that good feeling you have when your children and grandchildren are asleep under your roof. I tiptoed about, drinking coffee and thinking about them, and the minute I heard Susan stirring I was in her room with more coffee.

She is not a morning person, but she knows her home-coming obligation. It is to sit up in bed and talk to her mother who is propped up against the foot full of questions. When they live in faraway New Jersey and you haven't seen them in months, it's not as if you can push them up against the door-facing in the kitchen and take their measure.

You have to ask how much they've grown in all ways that children expand and develop. There's a lot you want to know and a lot you want to tell, and you laugh together and mull over mysteries inherent in little boys and girls, and it's warm and comfortable and very special.

I loved and enjoyed my other visitors, but a homecoming child of one's own is the best kind of visitor of all.

Mother's Day is one of those days I'm never ready for either. Neither physically nor emotionally. I mean to get myself together for the role of the matriarch of the clan, which my children assigned to me after the death of Muv. (I'm just keeping the post warm until Susy is old enough to take over. Unlike me, she is a born matriarch, firm of purpose, certain of her own infallibility.) But when they arrive in the country with their gifts I am likely to be wandering around blue-jeaned and barefooted with no plans or provisions for a gala meal and no inclination to be feted.

But they always come, if they are near enough for the trip, and they always "bring." Last year Mary worried that my loot was all stuff that needed planting.

"Maybe we should have brought something personal and ladyfied like dusting powder and perfume," she said.

"You're out of your mind," I said happily. "If I can't plant it, I don't want it. Besides, I've got a bottle of perfume and every time I smell it it gives me a headache."

They were great gifts, the rosebush, the yellow petunias, the gardenia to replace one the freeze took, the little shrub starred with fragrant yellow flowers.

But the real Mother's Day gifts were, of course, better than that. The baby, John Steven, soon to be a year old, clung to my finger and took brave but perilous steps across the terrace. I watched him try to walk alone, weaving uncertainly, big-eyed at his own temerity and a little triumphant, and then dropping to his all-fours to go scooting across the grass in pursuit of our dog, Stranger. He was taking the known way, his diapered bottom held high, his rosy face gleeful at the prospect of catching and kissing old Stranger.

Bless him, I thought. The best gift of all for Mother's Day or any day.

We took a little tub and a shovel and went back into the woods to look for moss for the wire hanging baskets and some wild ferns to transplant to the yard. David, the two-year-old, went with us, delighted to be ducking under bushes and climbing over logs.

The moss lining the sides of the little ditch looked

beautiful to him, and he squatted to inspect it and pat it. A little gray bird, undoubtedly frightened off her nest, whirred by his head, and he cried out in surprise and pleasure.

He wanted to help hold the shovel, which was two feet taller than he was, and he had to help carry the ferns, walking ahead of us into the clearing, the sun gilding his head.

Watching his sturdy little form trudging toward the garden path, I felt an unaccountable lump in my throat. The best gift, I thought again, the best of all Mother's Day gifts.

Later I rested my eyes on the brilliant red petunias as they swung lightly against the weathered gray boards of the toolhouse, and I thought about how the eldest of my grandchildren, John, had presented them to me.

He bought that basket on Saturday when I thought he had merely gone to get a haircut and perhaps add something to the unending supply of parts his car needs. He meant to present it on Sunday morning, but the responsibility of both hiding a big flamboyant basket of flowers and keeping it alive overnight weighed heavily upon him.

"I was gon' give you this tomorrow," he said gruffly. "But I didn't know what to do with it. So . . . here!"

He looked awkward and embarrassed over my cries of pleasure and gratitude.

"I don't know what you call 'em," he said, nodding toward the velvety blossoms. "The man said they were very healthy."

We got the ladder so he could hang it for me, and then there was a delay because he had to find some wire and pliers and extend the hanger. The length and breadth of him, a big redheaded boy with long arms and strong hands a little greasy from working on his car, poised on the ladder, holding the flowers, made me blink my eyes very fast. Yesterday he was a baby tottering over the terrace. Tomorrow he will be grown and gone.

But for that day ... ah, it's lovely to be eligible for Mother's Day!

The text of this book was set in Electra. The display is a photo typositor face, Novarese Book.

C. Linda Dingler designed the book and Jackie Meyer designed the jacket.

The book was composed by TriStar Graphics in Minneapolis, Minnesota, and printed and bound by Haddon Craftsmen, Inc., Scranton, Pennsylvania.